THE
CODE

THE
CODE

**Time-tested Secrets for
Getting What You
Want from Women—
*Without Marrying Them!***

Nate Penn and
Lawrence LaRose

A FIRESIDE BOOK

Published by
Simon & Schuster

FIRESIDE
Rockefeller Center
1230 Avenue of the Americas
New York, NY 10020

FIRESIDE and colophon are registered trademarks
of Simon & Schuster Inc.

Designed by BARBARA M. BACHMAN

Manufactured in the United States of America

1   3   5   7   9   10   8   6   4   2

Library of Congress Cataloging-in-Publication Data is available.

ISBN 0-684-84225-4

Contents

He knew that when he kissed this girl,
when he wed his unutterable visions to her
perishable breath, his mind would never
romp again like the mind of God.

— *The Great Gatsby*

The Code, like the great epics of yore, was never written down. Nor was it passed on by oral tradition. No one's grandfather ever told him about *The Code* on a fishing trip, or at a baseball game, or while instructing him in the occult mysteries of cabinetry. A man simply knows from birth that he must someday seek his fortune, his destiny, on the open road.

The open road is the realm of myth, of exile, of farmers' daughters. The open road is the territory Huckleberry Finn lights out for at the end of Mark Twain's novel. It's where Rabbit runs. It's the destination of poor, haunted David Banner at the end of every *Incredible Hulk* episode. It's Captain James T. Kirk's final frontier.

This book is a bugle call to arms (and legs; *long,* slender legs). It's a manifesto, an exhortation to

11

men everywhere. In these times of the *"Rules* girl" and the Sensitive Male, few of us remember any longer how to live by *The Code*. We need to reach out to each other. Whether you're Aeneas being tempted mid-quest by the coy Carthaginian queen Dido, or Paul Reiser earning his keep as TV's most emasculated house-husband, every man is an epic hero in the making. Every man must awaken to the responsibilities of *The Code*.

In the mid-1990s, lust has suddenly become a dirty word. A new breed of woman is hell-bent on dressing up sexual relationships in the Victorian fetters and snares her sisters once fought so heroically to break free of. She calls herself a *"Rules* girl,"* and if she has her girlish way, sexual politics will backlash to the Age of Cleaver.

In the wake of the sassy sixties, seventies, and eighties, a new age of covert gender operations has dawned. It's as if someone put Ronald Reagan and Ollie North in charge of the gender war.

In relationships as in life, it is the *Code* guy's nature—as Tennyson wrote—"to strive, to seek, to find, and not to yield." However heartbreaking each individual breakup in a *Code* guy's life may be, however much misery he may leave in his lonely adventurous wake, there is always the sense of a journey that must be made, the living potential of a great work in progress. Most of us, like our billions of dumb, microscopic, wriggling milky progeny, will not ever reach the terminal point of this journey. But as *Code* guys, we are helpless not to try.

Like the sperm he forges in the smithy of his scrotum, man is on a lifelong quest. Only one in a salty billion qualifies for the long haul; the rest are duds, dogs, and dawdlers. Through this journey's course, each man must restlessly pursue whatever eludes him, whatever challenges his imagination, whatever beckons from a distance—especially if she's backlit and wearing something sheer. So it has always been, so it shall always be: At the end of the day, a man desires nothing more than a furry place to keep his nose warm.

CHAPTER I

What Is *The Code*?

Simply, *The Code* is a time-honored set of behaviors and misbehaviors that guarantees fulfillment in your relations with women—without your having to sign binding legal agreements, miss a single Yankees game, or buy a Lexus' worth of precious gems. *The Code* shows you how to keep all your options open *all* the time, how to have a life of possibility with a capital P. Are we from Mars? We were skeptical at first, too. Read on!

How many times have you heard someone say, "He's sociable, he's handsome, he's smart . . . why is he *married?*" Could he have some as-yet-undetected character flaw, is he overcompensating, or is he the victim of a hoodwinking that would wow the Symbionese Liberation Army? Simply, how did a man of such promise fall to *this?*

Frankly, many men find it easier to cross continents, subdue natives, erect empires, or diversify mutual funds than to Just Say No to marriage. If you find yourself slipping, thinking nice thoughts of nuptials, then you need *The Code*.

Traditionally, *The Code* has been a tacit letter of intent among men, the unspoken agreement, the secret society, the worldwide Weltanschauung of noncommitment. It demands a written explanation, it demands this book, because of the cultural confusion find which we ourselves in. That is, at the same time that feminism has made sex more readily available and less confined to the padded cell of matrimony, there is also a growing army of sex-withholders, a radical band of women who want to play by the old rules. This book is a not-so-subtle assurance that we can answer (or not!) in kind. Many women believe anew that if they keep you hungry they are more likely to ensnare you—forever.

Pressure for wedlock marks a return to the Victorian schoolmarm's pinched morality. Commitment squanders the critical hunter-gatherer skills we are justly famous for. Without conquest, the open road meets a dead end; the journeyman becomes a "Fix Flats" nine-to-fiver. We're not talking hard to get, but impossible to pin down!

In a word, men and women are *different,* and it is important to pay attention to those differences so you don't get caught with your pants up. One major difference is that we don't communicate in

the same way women do; hell, we don't communicate at all if we can get away with it. We don't
recount last night's sex play-by-play, simply the
touchdown; we don't talk about *feelings,* simply
the touchdown. *The Code* will remind you when
to talk, what to talk about, and the fatal dangers of
plain speaking.

The Code is worldly advice, a realistic road
map, not some shadowy prescription for wish fulfillment and self-delusion. Plenty of people will
continue to sigh and speak of unions ordained on
high, but ask yourself a question: If this marriage
was made in heaven, why is everyone getting so
worked up about Tiffany's?

Many women would rather "ring" you into dependence, but a man stands or falls on his own
merits and meretriciousness while seeking his
own path. Even though each is on his own road,
there still have to be some traffic regulations. Well,
there's only one, if you really think about it: It is
verboten to pitch woo to another man's girlfriend—
all else goes. And even here, there is a disclaimer:
Should she voice her dissatisfaction, it is under-
stood that she has declared herself "in play."

Some will be wary that *The Code* is heartless
and insulting to women, and, well, if you're that
far gone we can't help you. But if you want to
enjoy the charms of the female sex without having to sign your life away, *The Code* is your *Fodor's*
to fornication.

A good friend of ours (since deceased) obeyed

The Code, and his life never lacked for adventure. Once a leader of a major Western power, he did as he pleased, flirted indiscriminately, threw his weight around fuzzy gnomic leaders of small islands, tweaked the noses of Mob bosses by bedding their wives, and even threw a star-studded party for himself where a Madonna lookalike (also since deceased) sang him "Happy Birthday." *Code* guy deluxe, he was the envy of the neighborhood. Still is.

Like our friend, adherents to *The Code* know full well that the half-life for any ecstatic relationship is roughly three months—the rest is just emotional fallout. Duck and cover! To put it another way, *The Code* means, on all levels, get in, get out, get in, get out.

Should you find your resolve crumbling, if you dream domestically of Crate & Barrel, if you muse unbidden about the charms of raking leaves and cleaning the gutters, thinking that *yes,* you *could* be happy with one woman for the rest of your life, read *The Code.* Read *The Code* more religiously than the Pentateuch. Immerse yourself entirely, remove yourself from the company of matrimonial namby-pambies, page through fashion magazines and stare at ads on the sides of phone booths, force yourself into tony bars packed with buxom Bambis, and, if you feel ready, buy our new video-cassette: "*Code* Calisthenics For Emotional Hardening" ($49.95).

Just remember not to overdo it—occasionally

you still have to affect a lust for kitchen appliances or you'll find yourself on a cold bus stop with no hope for any attention whatsoever for Mr. Winky. Men *do* have emotions; it is simply the smart men who know how to get rid of them, how not to fall to Cupid's curare.

So this is how it works: You've spent some time—maybe ten minutes, maybe two weeks—with a lissome beauty, and it doesn't look like she's heading for the door. What do you do? You *beware,* that's what you do! Don't get dealt the commitment card from the bottom of the deck! *The Code* states that if women seek commitment, we let them know that we are wildly, deeply, sincerely confused. Read *The Code,* and you'll know why you should never be so thickheaded as to feign commitment or testify too ardently.

You will learn how to *seem* supremely, manifestly focused on her, how to treat her like she's the only woman in the world (see Article VII: "How to Act on Dates 1, 2, & 3: Make Her Feel Like She's the Only Woman in the World"). Perhaps most critically, *The Code* will teach you: *Don't pay attention to what she says she wants, pay attention to what you know she wants* (see Article II: "She's Only After One Thing, and It Ain't Between Your Legs").

Hey! Don't over-think this! You may wonder: Should I tell her I love her? Should I make plans more than five hours in advance? Should I stop saying "I need my privacy"? Would she like to borrow my cellular phone for the weekend? Can I leave my golf clubs and fishing tackle at her place? Can I ever admit to cooking for myself?

The answer, stupid, is know *The Code*. Read *The Code,* be *The Code*. You can waste your time and try to think things through for yourself, but that's gonna cut into ESPN time, and then where will you be? It is easier to read *The Code:* It has always worked and, despite great cosmetic changes in sexual relations, always will. Try to navigate the shoals of modern romance, and you'll only Titanic yourself with too much thinking. Do what comes naturally: Be a Beast.

Every relationship can turn into a hostage crisis; don't be Jimmy Carter!

CHAPTER 11

Meet a Code Guy

Our friend Frankie is the antithesis of what is held up these days as the ideal man. He is in the Canadian Army Reserve (Special Forces), a part-time colonialist doing work for The Man and, dammit, he has killed people. Yes, killed people, unapologetically, and women love him.

Take a recent evening's dinner party as an example. Frankie served a palatable fusilli alla puttanesca, made a garden salad and, of course, whisked his own vinaigrette. He regaled our small gathering of eight with anecdotes in three languages, recounted battle plans from four wars and two "police actions," quoted Wordsworth and Auden, eagerly shared his dedication to a branch of western monotheism that keeps women in their place, and spoke of his pumping hot lead into irascible foreigners.

Plates were cleared, more guests arrived, hours passed. Somewhere around 2 A.M., when we were sipping Chablis and Rolling Rock, Frankie popped out of the kitchen with a tarte aux abricots, which he had summoned into existence with little more in the pantry than a stick of margarine and some leftover Smuckers. The women cooed. Later they couldn't stop speaking about his "character," his "determination," and his "worldliness." And his "commitment"; yes, that word again. Indeed, Frankie is a committed fellow: to his ideals, to his unit, and to the road. What didn't register, obviously, was Frankie's utter disregard for kneejerk bourgeois hallmarks: a home, a wife, rack-and-pinion steering.

Don't we all know a Frankie? Someone who feels right in his own skin; doesn't have qualms about doing what he wants to do, no matter how much he flies in the face of flaccid cultural mores? He's got a great shtick, and he sticks to it: he doesn't pine away the evenings complaining that his life is incomplete without a wife, that there's a gaping hole in his heart, or that there is a surplus of mindless women who throw themselves at him. You can see a Frankie on every corner. He's not the world's most handsome specimen, his pectorals don't rip through brushed cotton, he's not seven feet tall. He's an average guy with an above-average rate of success with women. Countless beauties want him to marry them, and he's let them all know that, some day, maybe, he will!

Because he is so hard to track down, we constantly get calls for Frankie's number. He is relentlessly on the move because he always has something *to do*. And Frankie's "something" isn't indiscriminate paper pushing or numbers crunching at some desk job which disgorges him promptly at five. No, Frankie travels the road between life and death, preaching the Western way with a colonialist's chutzpah, proselytizing with a semiautomatic, staring down hostile fire, and, in the process, defying every last P.C. sentiment ever uttered by Sally Struthers. Women can't get enough of him. Clearly, women are still attracted to men who are committed to the Big Three: God, Country, and Kalashnikov.

As our small dinner party made clear, Frankie doesn't seek women, chase after them like a lost poodle, or even ask them the first question. Women are acutely aware of who makes the first move, who asks first about the time or weather forecast, or who asks whom to dance. Frankie doesn't have time for such niceties and conversational frippery: He simply *is*.

By Frankie's very disavowal of the system of who asks whom first, he has turned the tables. He has women calling for *his* number. Of course he doesn't have time to return these calls immediately, creating an air of mystery: Could he be with another woman? Maybe he's in Djibouti? Or Dar es Salaam?

Initially we were stunned at his success

with beautiful women—eight-foot blondes, well-proportioned party girls, even the toxic debutantes(!)—especially in the face of our twisted attempts to be *nice guys*. We were, sad to admit, sincere, honest, and reliable. If we said we'd call, we called; we shared our feelings; we only mentioned other women when speaking of our days volunteering in an old folks' home. It got us nowhere; we were softies, lambs to the slaughter. We'd lost our religion; we had lapsed from *The Code*.

Seeing Frankie we realized all that we were missing, all that we had squandered in the arena of fair play, the disservice we were doing ourselves by maintaining a level playing field. There are asymmetries in nature, and we have reacquainted ourselves with them. We see that there is a basic imbalance to the sexes, and that's *The Code:* Keep them unbalanced!

CHAPTER III

But First the
Consumer—You!

Every market creates its own peculiar economy. The changing relationships of supply and demand result in almost constant price fluctuations. Any place where goods and services are exchanged sets up its own rate structures, patterns of exchange, and reasons for exploitation.

No different is Marx Bar, a meat-market single's spot not too far from our homes. Take a recent night as an example: Some impossibly Italian guy named Gianfranco—"No, really, call me Franco"—was all gold-chain wonderful and on the prowl, exercising a loose money policy—"Drinks for everyone"—that he thought would win him friends. Lucky for him, radiant Miranda wanted to be that friend. She sought to establish a welfare economy of sorts, flirting indiscriminately in a bold attempt to win over possible investors and then cross-sell her demure and less attractive friend Maureen.

"No, really, come meet my friend," she winked. Franco was all atwitter; the forecasts had been dismal, and then, suddenly, all the early indicators were proven less reliable than Laffer curves. "What a windfall," he said to himself, thinking thoughts of a three-way oligopoly. But Maureen didn't warm to the Roman, and Miranda strangely and swiftly cooled as well, disowning Franco in a sharp market reversal. Sadly, this rapid shortage in consumer goods reduced Franco to panic buying just before last call. He was forced to leave without any investment strategy whatsoever, later consoled only by his "invisible-hand" theory.

The lesson in all this, obviously enough, is that Franco didn't respect his market position: He's the *buyer,* for crissakes. The *Code* guy, by way of contrast, never forgets that he is, first and last, the consumer, and that is his strength. Women will try to manipulate the market by feigning scarcity— not returning calls, refusing more than one date a week—and thereby make themselves more desirable. But such artificial price supports ultimately frustrate domestic consumers (like you!) and encourage exchange with foreign ports—France, Sweden, Brazil (or Natasha, Sophie, Gabriella). Who the hell is going to be complaining about trade imbalance then?

Before you get caught in somebody else's Five-

Year Plan, it is imperative that you see what shapes the forces that create market satisfaction. Here's a primer on *Code* economy:

BOOM. You don't know what it is. Suddenly, with no shift in strategy, you're in a windfall. You've sown no seeds, and yet women are all over you like a thick sauce. Clearly, it's time to reap your profits—and reinvest.

BUST. Bust.

ECONOMETRICS. The stern study of the forces that undergird the market as a whole: fashion magazines, caloric intake, cosmetic improvements. The rocket science of romance.

EQUITY. Small money down against the larger house of love: the drinks date, FTD hellos, a dog (see Article XIV: "'You'll Never Love Me as Much as You Love That Dog': Canine Meditations").

FOREIGN AID. A costly, if potentially fruitless, endeavor. Nothing warms a woman's heart like foreign footwear: Buy her a pair of powder-blue Gucci loafers, and she'll be dropping her trade barriers faster than you can say C.O.D.

PENETRATION PRICING. She's new in town and hasn't a clue about prevailing rates. Intimidated by perceived market hostility from other pulchritudinous purveyors, she sells herself short, grossly undervaluing her purchase price. You're just the guy to show her a demand curve.

CREEPING INFLATION. You take her out for drinks. Both of you enjoy the evening. "Let's do it again soon." You do, and again, and then more frequently. Before you know it, your relationship is a drinking problem, and you're dizzy, punch-drunk, and penniless.

GALLOPING INFLATION. It was a nice drinks date and now she wants *what,* a horse farm? You've never in your life seen this sort of market acceleration.

FALSE ECONOMY. RuPaul.

CAVEAT EMPTOR. See "False economy."

PLANNED OBSOLESCENCE. *Code* guys—let's be frank—probably aren't what she really needs. But she doesn't know that yet, your marketing campaign was so impressive! With time your faults will come to the surface, and she'll wonder why she's moving your wares. Time to expand your economy.

STAGFLATION. Inexplicable, really. You've met her inflationary pricing, and she still wants to cut your nuts off. You don't *need* this job.

PAC-MAN DEFENSE. You smell a hostile takeover, so it's time to get hostile. Propose marriage and remind her that your pride insists any wife of yours is never going to lift a finger. Or leave the house.

POISON PILL. The writing is on the wall. She's enveloping you, and you don't know how to break free. "No," you say, "I don't necessarily want to separate, but I think I'd like to date around—with men."

BUY OR LEASE? If you're still asking yourself this question, you don't need the rest of this book, you need a CAT scan.

All history, to paraphrase Karl Marx, is an ass struggle, the tug-of-war between *Code*-guy venture capitalist and fiduciary would-be bride. She's trying to pull you over the line, and, for a time, you're willing to give minor commitment concessions. But when you find her suggested long-term hold undermining your bull market, it's time to let her know you're moving your entire portfolio into "Options." "You're wrong," she'll protest with a Black Monday foreboding, "you're wrong." Doesn't she know who she's talking to? Nothing could be further from the truth: The customer is always right.

ARTICLE I

BE A "BEAST"

A woman wants a man who bursts through the swinging doors of her heart's saloon like Clint Eastwood, an entourage of rolling tumbleweeds of pubic hair blowing in behind. She also wants to be memorialized by her man, to inhabit a world that is the physical manifestation of his love for her. She wants to be queen of a magic castle—like the one Bill Gates is devotedly building his new wife in the wilds of Seattle, in which the push of a button satisfies every desire. If you build it, she will come, and that means you will, too.

When Julia Roberts, winsome prostitute to Richard Gere's avaricious corporate-raider john in *Pretty Woman,* declares, on behalf of millions of American women, "I want the fairy tale," what does she have in mind?

We're thinking of a guy whose property holdings are a Martha Stewart wet dream: thousands of acres of impeccably tended French countryside crowned by a renovated medieval castle in which gourmet meals materialize out of thin air, tears metamorphose into tiny diamonds, and wardrobes are filled to bursting with shimmering silk designer gowns.

His girlfriend is one lucky chick, but she's understandably a bit overwhelmed. And she wonders why her dashing beau won't join her at the dinner table. But she gets along. The food is fabulous. Her bedroom is a wedding-cake fantasy out of one of those Hamptons summer showrooms. The clothes—to die for! And she's having such a good time flirting. But—hitch number 1—in the midst of these *Condé Nast Traveler* surroundings, she can't help but feel kind of guilty for abandoning her sick father.

There's a second hitch, too, and it's a biggie: She's Beauty in Jean Cocteau's *Beauty and the Beast,* and her boyfriend, the Beast, tends to interrupt their idyllic sylvan strolls to chase down grazing deer and devour them alive. Simply put, she worries he's too much of a beast for her.

Yet at the movie's conclusion, when the Beast is finally transformed into a blandly handsome, androgynous Prince Charming, our radiant Beauty feels an unexpected letdown. The Beast was such an interesting guy. He knew the names of all the trees and plants and munched on them with such relish. (Women love to watch men enjoy their food.) He was a divine horticulturist, and clearly his schlong, though as yet unsavored by her, was without peer. Why'd he have to turn into this loser male model guy? Where's that gorilla-faced sexual particle accelerator she fell in love with?

Greta Garbo, after viewing the film, famously declared, "Give me back my Beast," and who can blame her?

Every girl wants a beast. Sure, the medieval

French castle is probably beyond your means. So be a man of wealth and taste on your own terms. For the first three dates, anyway. Lay out some dough. Display a wide-ranging, if centimeter-deep, familiarity (like ours) with good books, good food, world history, philosophy, music, economics, the fine arts. But don't sweat the exam: Once you're past this first chat on world culture, you'll never, ever have another intellectual discussion with your girlfriend again. (It's a known fact.)

In a subsequent chapter, you'll find important *Code* tips on interior decorating (a small Oriental rug can work wonders) and *Code* cuisine (risotto, *sempre* risotto).

You've had two good dates at this point. It's time for her to pony up. Don't freak about the sex part, it's like what Erica Jong once wrote about dancing: Just move to the house jam, and the rest will take care of itself. Don't go changing to try to please the feminists and multiculturalists: *Code* guys know that few things are more gratifying than your girlfriend's burning lips at your ear whispering that you're the only real man she knows. We've been called animals many times, and it was always a compliment. Here are three thoughts to bear in mind:

1. No matter who she is, she always wanted to be one of *Charlie's Angels.* Give her a plum assignment. Past assignments have included: pom pom girl, porn star, lifeguard,

fashion model, beauty-show contestant, knife-thrower's assistant, ice-capades skater, white-trash biker, maid, real estate agent (before the boom: not cool), nurse, belly dancer, Southern belle, surrogate mother, prostitute, chorus girl, dope addict, roller-skating truck-stop waitress.

2. The best foreplay is a good meal followed by a massage. Just keep it relatively short or she'll fall asleep on you. If you're into role-playing, now is the time to pretend you're James Bond (women LOVE Sean Connery).

3. Your tongue is a Jeep Cherokee on the Dakkar-Paris 500. No part of her body is off-limits. After all, this is how cats clean themselves, and girls dig cats.

ARTICLE II

SHE'S ONLY AFTER ONE THING, AND IT AIN'T BETWEEN YOUR LEGS

We were on a pleasure quest one evening not too long ago, when merrily we happened upon an inn of indeterminate and potentially shady repute. No sooner had we made our way through the tumult and chaos of the pub crowd, when a short stocky fellow beckoned us on. We followed him through a labyrinthine set of back corridors to the Newt Room, which was, surprisingly, Newt-free.

But there was a vaguely Tibetan-looking fellow in a pair of Dockers, sitting on a case of Bud. "Symmetries can be deceiving," he hissed, in a comically ominous sort of way. Humored, we approached the ship-shape advice column to ask him what he meant. We fell easily into conversation on the question of circularity and eternal return, and he shared the Parable of the Ring and the Condom. "You put on a ring, and you never take it off," he said, touching forefingers to thumbs in a mock-Eastern seriousness to drive home his point, "but you put on a condom with the *express purpose* of taking it off!" Later that evening, we saw him ascend to an upstairs room, with a Moll Flanders/Alyssa Milano lookalike wrapped around him like a tarpaulin.

We mused at the bar that the Tibetan fellow's parable embodies the classic distinction between traveling for the sake of traveling and traveling to get to the inn. For the *Code* guy, the quest *is* the quest, of course, of course, no more and no less. If there's a Grail at the end, fine; but it's the striving, the test of manly mettle, that counts. For women, the dating journey aims for the inn and the wedding band—their Holy Grail.

So while she may coyly front you with her sultry desire for a "casual" relationship, don't think for a minute that it is anything but a staged performance devised to make you suspend your disbelief. Deep down, every groom should know that he's just the narrator in *Our Town,* seemingly everything, but really nothing more than a ringmaster marionette being tugged by the strings of some larger narrative not of his own making.

The French term *frisson*—at least we think it's French—refers to this shuddering realization, analogous to sitting in a dentist's chair, that the person next to you really doesn't have your best interests in mind. Your affair may seem like a droll farce or a naked stroll through the park, but keep this thought uppermost in your mind: All roads lead to Bed, Bath & Beyond!

ARTICLE III

WHERE THE GIRLS ARE:
   Sensible Shopping at the Meat Market

Beauty comes in two flavors, inner and outer, and women are always mixing new ingredients into the gazpacho of their selfhood. Theirs is an admirable, if sometimes neurotic, struggle, and in the end it often makes for a more interesting, complex dish. This Article focuses on *Code* nutrition: Below we present three locales where you can sniff what's cooking and, if you're so inclined, have a taste.

1. DEPARTMENT STORES

Women don't merely shop; they "go into" shopping, entering a stupefied trance of Zsa-Zsaesque rapacity and acquisitiveness. Today, she's buying tubes of bruise-colored lipstick; tomorrow, metallic nail polish that would shame the shine on a new Mercedes; the day after that, who knows? She's fickle, just like you; now you've discovered some common ground, and you might as well pick up some new socks in the men's department while you're there.

The best way to find a woman is to shop like one. Launch yourself into a fragrant, slowly revolving galaxy of cosmetics caddies and brassiere racks—all courteously orbited by fashionably attired women paid to talk to you. Can you stand it?

Unlike the epic protagonists of Dungeons & Dragons, however, you will require no magic knapsack filled with enchanted objects to serve you on your journey. For this daunting, dark voyage into the bowels of feminine consumerism, you need no pieces of gold, no magic staff, no ring of invisibility. Prepare to enter a forest primeval of hibiscus-scented moisturizers and cherry-bark conditioners.

You will call upon only one magic power on these libidinal adventures—that of the ever-replenishing *Code* imagination. Use it to fabricate the spectacularly large, extended female family you're shopping for: sisters, third cousins, nieces, mothers-in-law, recently widowed best-friends' wives. Follow the example of the Mafia hit man, whose unswerving affection for his mama redeems his odious enterprise: blanket your wolfish objectives in falsified consideration for other women.

If the effect of department store merchandise on women is narcotic (and it is), then salesgirls are the biggest dope-fiends of all. Surrounded daily by an unattainable vision of the good life, reduced to the meticulous wrapping-up of odd-shaped precious objects, bedazzled by too many zeroes, they are practically drugged into submission before you even approach them. No wonder they say "nice" all the time. They are the ultimate prisoners of the American Dream—and likely targets for *Code* cupidity. A salesgirl can't blow you off; you're a customer, and if you don't find what you're looking for, tomorrow's a new day. Place an order for some impossibly hard-to-find shade of eyeliner—cocaine, Granny Smith, Tetracycline yellow—and check in every day for the next four to six weeks.

2. THE GYM

To a *Code* guy, the gym is a modern-day temple dedicated to the perfectibility of the female form. Women apply themselves to the Stairmaster with religious fervor. Nowhere else will you find such plucky keisters. It's enough to make your teeth hurt (in a good way).

Unlike most *Code* methods of seduction, working out actually has a primary benefit for you. The physique of a man who sits around all day long, plotting and devising, can bear an unfortunate resemblance to the Stanley Cup. You don't want her hoisting you triumphantly aloft. You better work!

Know that even feminism's changing of the gender guard hasn't displaced raw muscular power from the pantheon of male virtues. She won't be impressed if you ask her to spot you. Nor will she be fooled if you double-bag your reedy biceps in layers of sweatshirts. There's always somebody bigger than you, and at the gym there are about forty of those somebodies, well-oiled Atlases of every ethnic stripe, each credibly impersonating the Brooklyn Bridge amid a complex cross-hatching of cables and wires that recalls nothing so much as Duchamp's unfinished installation *The Bride Stripped Bare by Her Bachelors, Even*. Have you lost your way and wandered into Vulcan's forge?

If, in the end, your blue ox Babe decides to attach herself to one of these Paul Bunyans instead of you, take comfort on two fronts: (1) Your penis is probably bigger than his; and (2) All they're going to talk about, ever, is power-lifting.

3. ART HISTORY

Whether collegiate or adult ed, art history classes are where the action is—and we don't mean Jackson Pollock's action painting. Stop & Shop Singles Night is no place to meet a muse: The truly avant-garde babes are all in "Twentieth Century Art," their pink pencil erasers tapping absently against their pearly teeth.

What does this say about women, and—more important—how can you exploit it to your advantage? Are women more visual than men? A billion dollars' worth of pornography, most of it rented by Clarence Thomas, says no. Are they more artistic? Think of the picture-perfect breasts you taught yourself to sketch in junior high, and the answer has to be a (boastful) uh-uh.

Art history class is the *Mirabella* of the female intelligentsia, offering a given historical era's worth of fashion dos and don'ts under the legitimizing aegis of higher education. Your female classmates are nothing but supermodels of the mind, sashaying down the intellectual runway sporting blithe allusions to Fragonard (the guy who gave John Galliano his bustles), Malevich (a likely inspiration for the palette of Calvin Klein's recent fall collection), and the Cubists (that brilliant, *brilliant* Issey Miyake). The first time one of these women opens her mouth to speak in class (presumably to advance the cause of Western thought), you halfway expect fifty prepaid subscription mailers to tumble out.

If all this sounds intimidating—and any remark does when it's delivered in a French accent from behind a pair of tiny, sixteen-sided spectacles—

bear in mind that this mode of feminine self-improvement, like all the others, is arranged for you. Don't despair when your early forays in flirtation are met with an indifference such as you have never known before; even Nurse Ratched is more receptive to male blandishments than the implacable art squad. There is simply no variety of woman harder to impress. How do you do it, then?

Diligently apply yourself to watching Elsa Klensch, the lockjawed doyenne of cable fashion programs, and her school of imitators: *Videofashion! Weekly, Fashion Television.* There are worse punishments: You'll never see so many nipples without paying for premium cable. Plus the breasts are real, and the women are either weird-looking or luminously gorgeous—never ugly. Watch obsessively, as we do, and in no time you, too, will be chatting about the impeccable tailoring of a Richard Tyler blazer. Whatever that means. You'll get the hang of all this soon enough, and once you do, you can mute the sound and do something really useful with yourself.

ARTICLE IV

LET'S MEET FOR DRINKS: *The Non-date Date*

Today's liberal social mores have sanctioned the presence of women in bars and made it possible, even advisable, to seduce them in plain sight. Indeed, the very proposition of "having drinks" with a woman carries with it a sophisticated metropolitan tang, a Cheeveresque sophistication. There's nothing shameful about it. Which is quite amazing, given that what you're getting her to enact symbolically is the intimate exchange of tart fluids you have planned for later that evening (as well as the spiking of said fluids).*

Meeting for drinks is the sample slice of salami at the Balducci's meat counter, the representative strawberry from the open basket. It's the test drive of dates: Some will go from zero to sixty in 6.2 seconds, others will never make it out of the garage. How do you know what kind of buggy you're driving together unless you go for a spin?

Unfortunately, on first meeting, a woman trusts a man about as much as an Orthodox Jew trusts Saddam Hussein. You may gaze longingly at the borders of her small, fertile, vagina-shaped country, but she has committed herself resolutely to its staunch defense. She knows all about your SCUD missiles and your armies of the night, and unless you're willing to grow earlocks and invest in black haberdashery, she's not going to issue you

---

* Theorists may debate the flavor tones various drinks impart to your semen—the fruity astringency of an Alabama Fizz versus, say, the flowery treble notes of a Biffy Cocktail or even the misty vanilla nose of a Bosom Caresser. It's truly a considerate *Code* guy who solicits a short list of his date's preferences.

a visa anytime soon. To her, you are a vile, unclean thing—a pig, a clam, not a man. A *Code* goy.

The best news about this first meeting is that you're not getting any. Any money from the cash machine, that is. Nor are you expending a great deal of your valuable time. In this brief first negotiation, this short opening volley in the battle of the sexes, you bring as little to the table as possible. But you do make one concession—to have the meeting on her turf. Women feel safer in public, so you take her to a public place. In turn, she acquiesces to your loose construction of the word "public," applied by you exclusively to activities with an extremely low price tag.

You know what to say during your non-date date: namely, nothing (see Article V: "Don't Talk—Let Her Project"). Women like looking at things that don't talk, whether it's *Les Demoiselles d'Avignon,* designer kitchens, shoes, or beach houses. Silence is to women as Vivid Video is to men—a veritable cottage industry of the libidinal imagination.

But SAY nothing doesn't mean DO nothing. You will have undertaken a study of your own facial musculature that makes Marcel Marceau look like a bust of Lenin. Your eloquence is all in the ambiguous shadings of your features—enhanced by the lighting of the bar, which you've scouted in advance. You are Mr. Chiaroscuro, and you, like Madonna and Rita Hayworth, give good face. Here are the basic tactics you will need to employ on a drinks date:

1. *The tight-lipped smile.* A complex and sophisticated expression revealing your seriocomic sensibility. (Also conceals free hors d'oeuvres stuck in your teeth, should you have any such concerns.) Has a rueful quality that will signify you've caught the irony in what she's saying. Keep it sufficiently mysterious so that, if you weren't supposed to smile to begin with, it's OK.

2. *Mirroring.* The better part of charm is slavish imitation. On a non-date date, mirroring is a quick and easy way to subliminally establish that you're soulmates: After all, you've struck exactly the same pose from the waist up. Without knowing why, she will feel obscurely comforted. She may even find herself wondering how your bodies would fit together. (You've already figured that one out.)

3. *The narrowed gaze.* The look that says, "Ouch." An effective means of conveying sympathy when she's talking about a horrible accident that has befallen someone you've never even heard of.

4. *The lip-bite (top front teeth/lower lip).* A playful acknowledgment that something a tad risqué has just transpired. Effectively implicates her in your love conspiracy,

luridly illuminates the night in 42nd Street neon. A tactic that's most effective if she already likes you a little; anyway, you won't want to try it too often because—its effects notwithstanding—it makes you feel like a total fool.

5. *Cupped chin with extended finger on nose.* You are very engaged with what she is telling you. In fact, you may be about to say something. Except that you're not.

Above all, keep the non-date date short. You are a mighty night train filled with a precious cargo, and there are many stops yet to make; others are waiting. Whenever possible, practice boxcar non-dating, in which you link one short drinks engagement to another and another and another, and so on, and so on, rattling forward, ever thrusting, churning, pumping, deep into the good *Code* night.

ARTICLE V

DON'T TALK—LET HER PROJECT

In Woody Allen's *Bullets Over Broadway,* John Cusack is not the great playwright he pretends to be. Every time he tries to explain the truth to Dianne Wiest, his leading lady and worldly-wise lover, she forces his mouth shut, commanding him:

"Don't speak!" Every woman preserves her illusions in her own way. Just don't interfere. What she prefers is to connect your dots. Submit to the Crayola of her imagination. But how?

A spate of recent books—including bestsellers like *When Elephants Weep* and *The Hidden Life of Dogs*—invest our nonverbal animal neighbors with noble human qualities they may not possess at all. Consider that a homeless guy who politely asks for money is far less likely to win our sympathy than a squirrel with its paws upraised in mute pleading. Silence, like the retriever, is golden. You're a Beast, remember? Keep quiet, let her anthropomorphize you, and you're halfway home.

Animals are our confidants from earliest youth. We project the best qualities of our souls onto them: devotion, bravery, innocence. Sometimes when we pet them we get into sort of a rhythm and can't stop, and it's kind of like, well, masturbation. We can't imagine our pets ever doing anything *really* bad—certainly nothing more heinous than the petty crimes of poor bowel control or hunger run amok. Think about it: No one ever accused the Akita of offing Nicole and Ron, and he was found at the crime scene with four bloody paws!

We imbue our confessors—pets, priests, psychiatrists—with insight and judgment. How else are they supposed to make sense of our twisted lives? The shrinks call it "transference." *Code* guys call it the mother lode of seduction. Mine it. Let a woman talk uninterrupted for a spell, and she will invest you with the compassion and wisdom of Bishop Tutu and the sensuous abandon of The Artist Formerly Known As Prince.

But if you speak, the jig's up. She'll know instantly who she's dealing with. In disguising his dark and ambiguous motives, the *Code* guy's dilemma is not unlike the one that confronted the animators of the recent cartoon adaptation of Victor Hugo's classic novel: Namely, how do you make a hunchback cute? Emulation of adorable and mute animals offers a ready-made solution. Two options are available to the animal-mimicking *Code* guy:

1. *Dogs.* From the stoic bravery of Lassie, to the haughty indolence of Snoopy, to the athletic exuberance of the Golden Retriever in *Independence Day*—who vaults over a car to escape a tunnel-borne fireball—dogs embody simple, direct, all-American virtue. Their well-established rectitude (founded on many life-saving acts of courage) empowers them to indulge their carnal desires with enviable frankness. If only YOU could saunter into a room and instantly begin humping the most attractive woman in it.

    But at the end of the day, dogs aren't human beings, and women (well, most women) won't sleep with them. Perhaps this explains the infinite sadness we sometimes see in their (the dogs') eyes. (Stop us if we're projecting.) Which is where you have a leg up—so to speak.

Master the attentive ear-perk; the gaping, toothsome smile; the intrepid crotch-sniff. Your date will infer qualities you never knew you possessed (because you don't): heroism, loyalty, generosity. Meanwhile, your craven hunger for sex thoroughly dispatched with. Is this wh like to be Axl Rose?

2. *Cats.* The dispossessed European n the domestic animal kingdom, the ultimate *Code* animals. Haughty, obscurely preoccupied with son unpaid debt, cats make no pro no explanations. They just lie Sphinxes of self-absorption, utter slothfulness. What th of them? And yet womer Try imitating a cat some actually enlist someon you each day, then ch your tightly compac you don't need thi

Animals can turn a v bert. They're all on gaze on them just

give it up good. Forget Andrew Marvell's seventeenth-century pick-up routine where he tells the girl she should shoot the satin rapids with him straightaway, time's wingèd chariot is hurrying near, etc., etc. Had Marvell simply kept quiet, he'd have been more sexually satisfied. After all, writers only write to get laid (present company not excluded).

Greek myth tells us that the god Epimetheus was so generous in endowing animals with the virtues of strength and swiftness and grace and courage that there was little left over for man. You'll find no argument here.

Table I
Famous Code Guys

The young Augustine
Henry Miller
John F. Kennedy, Sr.
Kramer
Norman Mailer
Frank Sinatra
Daniel Day-Lewis
Mark Antony
Dennis Rodman
early Ralph Reed
Ernest Hemingway
Sean Connery
Dean Martin
Jack Nicholson

John Huston
Onan
Bill Clinton
John McEnroe
Mark Messier
Axl Rose
Matt Dillon

ARTICLE VI

HOW TO ACT ON DATES 1, 2, & 3:
Make Her Feel Like She's the
Only Woman in the World

Where you bring a woman on a date will largely shape her early impressions of you. A date's ambience—its lighting, its location, its cuisine; in short, how expensive the restaurant is—speaks volumes to her about how you live, or want to live. Also about how long you'll wait for sex.

Dates are fashion shows, sensuous (we hope), strutting processions of our latest selves. The tailoring of every date is different, but behind the scrim, in the minds of the participants, every date is exactly alike. We all want to sell our collection.

In some cases, a date results in a serendipitous fitting of her tastes and inclinations with yours. But all too often, the upshot is a horrendous clashing of the colors of your identities.

Below we outline a sequence of three dates

honed to perfection by a fleet of poorly paid but highly gratified *Code* field workers. Of course, it's never possible to guarantee success in the capricious world of couture, but if you expend the time and effort you're usually going to end up with something quite nice. Even if you only wear it once.

DATE 1: THE ESTÉE LAUDER

A fresh, innocent, daytime date, often conducted outdoors in a floral setting, the Lauder establishes you as a very dashing and courtly young man. You begin the proceedings by picking her up at her place. After a succinct, witty, and admiring comment on the decor (delivered in an English accent, if you can manage it), you proceed to the park, equipped with country loaf, jug of wine, and wedge of Stilton. Once seated on checkered picnic blanket, you blithely recite Wordsworth for her and hum your school song. When a kindly old man passes by on a creaky Raleigh, you hail him cheerfully and press him for a brief loaner. You seat your date on the handlebars and cycle together laughingly in a slow, gallant circle.

At date's end, you are both still breathlessly atwitter, but you compose yourself long enough to pay for her cab. You kiss her hand goodbye and, while pushing back your flowing hair from your forehead and succumbing to a series of marvelously appealing facial tics, you tell her you think you're falling in love.

DATE 2: THE TODD OLDHAM

In loose, colorful, yet subtly muted garb, you mumble across the table over shrimp-and-sweet-potato burritos, in a high-ceilinged, creative tapas bar in the warehouse district. Using only a napkin, her lipstick, and the water from the table carafe, you construct a colorful wrap for the nearly empty glass bottle of olive oil you spied on her kitchen counter. Now it's a funky flower vase for that bouquet of yellow tulips you brought her from the corner Korean! You have a couple of drinks—sweet and sophisticated, perhaps Absolut Citron on the rocks—and casually mention you're going to a wedding in the next couple of weeks. You're really excited: You haven't danced in so long!

DATE 3: THE GALLIANO

Your voice has a rasp to it she hadn't noticed before, and your eyes glitter in the light of the black candle stub on the table. Behind her rises the five-foot-tall, potted white orchid you brought her from Maxim's. (It's shaped like a pudenda.) Before dinner even arrives, you polish off a bottle of bloody red wine together. The food is richly delicious, all of it lacquered with a decadently pricey cognac demiglace. She doesn't quite understand what you're saying—you're speaking urgently, in a mixture of English, French, and Russian—but you keep mentioning guillotines; you make vague accusations against your coachman. Suddenly, in a passionate gesture, you take her hands in both of yours. (How is it possible that your fingers are storming her thighs at the same time?) You wrap her in your velvet cloak and silently whisk her into the nearest available cab. The streets are empty of spies; in the bedroom of her chateau, a great social upheaval ensues. She brings out the peasant in you.

ARTICLE VII

DATES 4 THROUGH RIPCORD:
You're Always in a Meeting

Date 3 went well. *Real* well, you like to think. All that you had hoped for was consummated in fantastic furbelows of unclothed abandon, rustling and tussling through the silken landscape of her four-poster. What could be better? In a word, plenty. You've gained her trust and made her feel like she's the only woman in the world—you even told her "she's a creature unlike your mother"— and now it's time for something more.

The hard work you've put in—the hand-pressed shirts, the candle-lit dinners, the *honesty*— has provided sufficient security for her to acknowledge, if only shyly, that her desire has become unanchored. You're ready to lift off together for fabulous heights of cloud-scraping lust, aided and abetted by the rocket-fuel of risotto (see Article XI: "Reviving Aphrodesia: *Code* Interior Decoration and *Code* Cuisine"). As long as your high-flying appetites hold sway, every date is date 4.

But comes a day when the cloth of your mutual concupiscence becomes threadbare, faded, and indistinct. Slowly, you realize your lust has been transformed into something decidedly off-the-rack, the designer passion of your former selves slipping into the Macy's of love and, eventually, excruciatingly, the Gap. What has happened to her? The form-fitting Alaïa cocktail dresses that won her to you have been replaced with a wardrobe's worth of Laura Ashley knock-offs. Was it something you did, or has she moved into a new color palette of subtly hostile asexuality? Worse still, her sweetly off-color pronunciamentos of passion have been supplanted by the boilerplate language of feminine affection: marriage, baby names, school districts. It's not date 4 anymore.

You can play her game; you have before. If you won her over with Savile Row suits and silk ties, you can just as easily turn her off with worn cotton-poly sweatpants and Carhartt jackets. Clothes make the man, and you're now in the process of unmaking hers. Wrap yourself in barn jackets and sing the praises of permapress shirts; mute astonishment will quickly replace her matrimonial mus-ings. The wayward sartorial gesture certainly won't be sufficient to drive her off your scent; it's going to take some work. Fancy clothes and ac-coutrements won her attentions; you're going to have to go down market, bud, way down.

Strike a lowly pose: Tell her you've landed a job at LaGuardia as a runway traffic controller and proudly display your brilliant orange jump suit. You can't believe you haven't discovered these things before. "Isn't it functional? See how it zips?" Wear it all the time.

When she calls you at work, intimate darkly about "the job" and tell her you haven't time to talk now, you have to get into "a meeting." Her piqued curiosity will greet you the next time you speak. In whispers, tell her about your great plans for the two of you, once the "Lufthansa job" is pulled off. Of course she shouldn't discuss this with anyone (least of all her therapist), but you're brimming with hope; you couldn't not tell her. Does she mind if you store a couple of bags at her place tomorrow night? You rush to hang up—"the meeting's start-ing"—before she has a chance to respond.

Your whistling descent is almost audible; no one has fallen in her eyes so far, so fast. What did she ever see in you? Who do you think you are, involving her in this activity? At first she thinks it's sexy to risk something illegal, but then realizes what marrying her fate to yours really means: She can't get hold of you at work, and you're a *lousy* dresser. How could she possibly have thought *you* would provide a good home for her children? Beats you.

HOW TO MEET THE RELATIVES

Don't.

THE ONLY MESSAGE IS A MIXED MESSAGE

Of all the *Code*-guy arts, the mixed message is perhaps most sublime. Like the Greek god Hermes, who experienced sex as both a man and a woman, the mixed message, when ingeniously concocted, has it both ways: It seems to satisfy her interests, when in fact it is all about satisfying yours, big-time. The mixed message takes the long view, understands that every relationship is just a detour from the Route 66 of possibility. If the mixed message were a part of speech, it would be an adverb named "maybe."

A four-star mixed message usually takes the form of some assurance on a critical relationship issue: "How do I look?" "Why won't you take me to St. Kitts?" "Do you love me?" (a query so rich in its possibilities for subversion that it has its own chapter in this book). A mixed message's latent purpose, of course, is to sow a wildly fertile seed of doubt in your partner's mind. This is a hardy little seed indeed, one that thrives in all seasons and requires very little maintenance. (All it requires to bloom into full-blown paranoia is the occasional administration, every day or two, of more mixed messages.) So practice and devise and hew to this all-important article of *The Code.* In time, and with experience, you, too, will develop a green thumb for the seed of doubt.

To get you started, we present you with a half dozen exemplary, field-tested mixed messages:

1. *You would if you had the money.* The all-purpose answer when your girlfriend asks you why you never take her on vacation, or buy her romantic gifts, or pay for a cab when she goes home. At first, she will sympathize; it's no fun having no money, everybody knows that. She'll remind herself that she didn't choose you for your money in the first place. In fact, she may even ruefully pride herself on it.

   But with enough repetition of this particular refrain, she'll soon remember what the road to hell is paved with (hint: good intentions). You can count on her friends to furnish the bass line to the torch song of her discontent by observing that your behavior fits "a pattern." Assuming she is a reasonable person, your girlfriend will inevitably conclude as follows: Maybe you would if you had the money, maybe you wouldn't. The more relevant point is, you don't and you're not. She's young, and she should be having fun. She deserves better. She's right; you have to admit it, she's right.

2. *X-traordinary ex-girlfriends.* When she teasingly inquires about the women who came before her, have short, terrifying anecdotes at the ready: "Serena never went to the gym, she was naturally toned"; "Madeline made the greatest risotto— she'd just pop it on the burner, jump in the shower and it was done"; or "Catherine was a dancer, a French ballerina, actually."

   If you're not a verbal kind of *Code* guy— and few of us are, let's face it—the action corollary of this mixed message is to buy lingerie for her that's either too big or too small, depending on the item ("Oops, that was Madeline's size"). A further addendum: Lingerie stores are truly the candy store of the *Code* guy libido. Nowhere else can you request that a salesgirl strip to the underwear of your choice. Just remember, no tipping!

3. *Playing the race card.* Take her aside and let her know you have something important to

tell her—that your friends think she's a racist. Emphasize that you defended her strenuously.

4. *Savvy dealmakers: Pitching the ménage à trois.* Her friend Sophy is a raven-haired, electric, Catholic-school-girl-gone-bad, dead ringer for Alyssa Milano. Ninety-nine out of a hundred men would drag their tongues ten city blocks in the hope of eventually meeting up with one of her bare toes. Following your first meeting with Sophy, you will be asked if you think she is pretty. Not extremely, you say, and shrug. Your girlfriend may not believe you, but she won't challenge you, either. In fact, she'll feel incredibly sorry she ever asked: She damn well knows the answer to her question, and at this point, she certainly doesn't want to hear it from the likes of you.

Sometime later, in a moment of post-coital indolence, she asks if you'd like to try "something different" sometime. You might, you say shyly. What, she asks, with a seductive feline stretch. Sophy, you say. But wait: You didn't think Sophy was pretty! True, you say; Sophy's sexy, not pretty. Should your girlfriend's poise desert her at this point, you can remind her that it's only a fantasy; anyway, she asked. A person can't be blamed for their fantasies. Or their honesty. The next day, suggest inviting Sophy over for fondue.

5. *I've never broken up with anyone.* Modestly acknowledge your singular track record of domesticity, reliability, contentment, and commitment. Express anxiety that you'll get done in again. Later, you will confess that even though they all broke up with you, every one of your previous girlfriends was married. An introspective person, you worry about what this might say for your own capacity for intimacy.

6. *You look* [pause pause pause] *nice.* Ta-da! She's just shown you the clothes she's picked out for the evening. (Be advised: If you really want to get out of the apartment that night, use a different tactic.)

ARTICLE X

THE ONLY RULES ARE YOUR RULES: *Discuss Like a Democrat, Lead Like Attila*

Although you've worked to hone your skills of in-decision—with rapid reversals of direction and infinite deferrals of answers to simple questions—

you should maintain a firm goose-stepping leadership when it comes to outings with your girl. By all means, solicit ideas, welcome suggestions, and entertain possibilities. Then do what you had in mind in the first place. In short, talk like a Democrat; don't be one.

Many politicians get a lot of play out of "town meetings," those cheery communal gatherings that spark debate, articulate hope, vent frustration, and typically produce nothing they didn't start with. Try holding your own town meeting for two: Work the rooms of your apartment like Jenny Jones on Dexatrim; needle your girlfriend; encourage her to say what's really on her mind, what course she thinks you should follow together. Then pretend the meeting never took place. Man your ship of state as it ought to be manned—manfully.

No woman will respect you if you're wishy-washy, committee-minded, and deferential. "How will he survive in the real world?" she'll ask herself. "Won't he be run over roughshod?" "He says he's an alpha-male, but why's he always stuck in the longest grocery checkout line?" Even Sylvia Plath conceded, with sobering frankness, that every woman loves a Fascist. So strive to emulate Mussolini—or at least the Lion King—if you have any randy designs on what's beneath her brown skirt.

If you don't impose your will, she'll smell weakness. Simple questions like, "Which movie do you want to see?" can form a beachhead of suspicion in her mind if you don't emphatically answer, *"Terminator,* dammit." Bungled and belabored discussion only creates resentment more free-floating than the game piece on a Ouija board.

To avoid such conversational cul-de-sacs, study the masters of iron will. Surprisingly, the gentlemanly sport of tennis has supplied some great leaders in this hallowed male tradition. Tennis players whine and plead and heatedly disavow anything that contradicts their vision of the world, no matter how plain and obvious the error of their ways. In turn, they are handsomely rewarded, pampered, and chased by legions of luscious babes. Learn from them.

For instance, John McEnroe typified all that was good about forceful negotiation. Was he hamstrung by the prevailing and pigheaded reverence of linesmen? Was he handcuffed by consensus? Hell no! He made his own calls.

It is important to be able to see the world only as you wish. En route to your goal, it is essential to master the skill of saying one thing and doing another. Louis "The Charmer" Farrakhan (so named for his suave success as a calypso singer in the 1950s) exhibits a fixity of purpose that few mere mortals can muster: He'll say *anything* to achieve his goal. Then he'll say he never said it.

Any *Code* guy desperately facing dwindling prospects at party's end can appreciate the Farrakhan switchback. What you said under the duress of last night's bacchanal is always re-

----

tractable in the light of day splashing across her coverlet. "Respect you in the morning? I *did* drink too much."

Remember, discuss like a Democrat, *do not* act like one. Mimic the conversational strategies of Clinton—engaged, informed, charming—but don't lead like him. He is the Mobius strip of indecision, twisting back on himself infinitely: Clinton leading Clinton, without ever getting anything done, stuck forever in the whiff of wrongdoing, but never actually stopping to check the bottoms of his shoes. A modern Hamlet, Übermensch of fence-sitting and mugwumpery, he never confidently thrusts his sword toward that for which he is truly jonesing. It's his wife who's Attila.

TABLE II
"OURS GO TO ELEVEN";
ELEVEN QUICK TAKES ON GETTING IN
& GETTING OUT OF A RELATIONSHIP

GETTING IN	GETTING OUT
1. Cook risotto for her.	Promise risotto; hot dogs instead, no buns.
2. Take her to fancy restaurant where you know the owner.	Take her to tourist-trap Italian place and spill cheap red wine on her Isaac Mizrahi dress.

GETTING IN	GETTING OUT
3. Introduce her to famous or powerful or accomplished people you know.	Introduce her to your friends.
4. Champagne after the first time you make love.	Drink all the cranberry juice in her refrigerator.
5. Rent classy movies with strong female protagonists: *Breakfast at Tiffany's, Belle de Jour, Smiles of a Summer Night*.	Rent pornography on her video-store account and keep it till the store calls her.
6. Wake her up with oral sex.	Wake her up with your morning erection; suggest that she "hop on."
7. Massage her feet with Lubriderm.	Clip your toenails over the kitchen sink.

GETTING IN	GETTING OUT
8. Bite the buttons off her blouse the first time you make love to her.	Bite the buttons off her blouse every time you make love to her.
9. Express sexual desire for aging feminist icons (Lauren Bacall, Barbra Streisand).	Express sexual desire for Dominique Moceanu.
10. Take her to see Janeane Garofalo.	Take her to see Andrew Dice Clay.
11. Take her to Tanglewood in May.	Take her to a Jets game in December.

ARTICLE XI

REVIVING APHRODESIA:
Code *Interior Decoration* and Code *Cuisine*

Like necromancers, astrologers, and alchemists, *Code* guys realize that although hard work has its own pay off, relying on philtres, amulets, and charms is a lot more fun and a shortcut to seductive stupefaction. Interior decorating and cooking are both occult practices, enlightened ministrations aimed at summoning something eternal and inspired out of what, soberly examined, are really just threadbare throw pillows and market vegetables.

Enshrouded in heavenly and intoxicating unguents, perfumes, and pomades, women silently exert a forceful, albeit subliminal, pull on the male libido. For his part, the *Code* guy has his own arsenal of smells: So what if they are all in your apartment? The ripe scents that emanate from your quarters speak *you,* and speak you loudly.

You do not truck with normal hygiene, yet your odoriferousness exerts an insistent and primal tug on your enamored's libido. The challenge is just getting her within whiffing distance to unleash the magic. Proudly, you live in filth; every room has its own special reek of mysterious origin and composition, something decomposing here, something unwashed there. Her first step into your lair is a deep plunge into a sea of free-floating pheromones; you shouldn't be surprised by a spontaneous discussion of unplanned pregnancies.

The *Code* guy knows how to put the best face on things. If time doesn't permit you to think for yourself, here's some help to give your rat-trap the charm of Cézanne's atelier:

What She Sees	What You Call It
coffee mug, ringed from repeated use	"the chalice"
beer bottle under bed	"objet trouvé"
leaky radiator	"the samovar"
jocks hanging from a rusty nail	"swags"
three weeks' worth of dishes stacked next to sink	"interactive installation" (especially if she washes them)
crumbs on floor	"manna"
Ernest & Julio Gallo boxed wine (3 liters)	"the jeroboam"
asbestos-like execrescence bulging from wall	"bas-relief"
newspapers occluding floor	"floor treatment"
Coleman lantern on your nightstand	"the torchère"

What She Sees	What You Call It
centerfolds of Alyssa Milano, Pamela Anderson Lee, and Jenny McCarthy pasted to your bedroom ceiling	"the triptych"

THE ALCHEMY OF SEDUCTION

A good risotto, like a successful consummation, is a quasi-philosophical endeavor, a meditation on identity, a convergence of multiple influences. Particular to arborio rice is its power to bind and take on the flavors around it, commingling essences in the transformation from pellets of starch to a succulent climax of the senses.

Sensitive to the average man's disinclination to do one thing well when he can do two things half-assed—to say nothing of the fact that we know you left this to the last minute—this recipe incorporates the proper preparation of a truly mystical risotto and a pretty good you:

Risotto with Clams and Asparagus, No Time to Lose

1 pound asparagus,* erect, though trimmed

2 dozen littleneck clams,* the tightest you can find, showered

4 tablespoons extra virgin olive oil*

1 large onion,* hacked, chopped, and generally obliterated

2 cloves garlic,* mashed

2 cups arborio rice,* *imported* (Jersey does *not* count)

2 mouthfuls dry white wine*

salt* to taste (*your* taste)

pepper*

1 4/5 tablespoons chopped parsley*

Galvanize soggy spirit. Summon heat from beneath 5-quart pot generously supplied with H_2O. Lavish towel on head: Swab ears, back, and legs; throw on boxers. Wait.

Introduce asparagus into boiling ablution, lightly salted. Tweak nose hairs and dispatch with unibrow. Wait some more, forestall mad hope, and remove spears after 4 to 5 minutes. Reserve broth. Set spears aside to cool and sever top (gently!).

Tickle underarms with deodorant, set aside. Reduce heat under broth with gentle pleading. Busy self with clams. Defile bivalves in covered pan over high heat in waist-deep salted water. Caress teeth

* Indicates a recognized aphrodisiac.

with floss and fluoride. Return to now-opened clams, remove salty rations from virginal residences and set aside. Slip on pants, belt, and left sock.

In separate reliable vessel over medium heat, impassion olive oil against sublimation, and add onion. Warm to pellucidity and acquaint with garlic. Wrap self in cashmere turtleneck (black). Usher asparagus stalks into pot and bring the oily admixture to their notice. Nudge intimately until a lightly gilded sheen is realized.

Pluck up heart, herald the concupiscent climax: Add rice.

Stir vigorously with long wooden spoon and moisten with wine. Stir. Reverse turtleneck (you put it on backward). Stir. Engorge rice with additional 1/2 cup of simmering broth. Continue to dexterously abet commingling of solid and liquid. Stir. Slowly introduce 1/2 cup of broth, continually caressing sides and bottom until liquid is drawn in. Answer door. Stir, stir, pepper, stir. Add broth, stir. Sneak into bedchamber for other sock and shoes. Return.

Launch clams into hot arborio hell. Offer her* a drink,* asshole! Continue to cook until rice is tender but firm. Transfer to serving platter. Sprinkle profligately with parsley, invoking Rabelais: "It grows for the wicked but not for the just."

Light candles. Serve with vigor and dispatch. Devour and seduce (either order—you choose) in hazy romantic glow, your contact lenses in the wrong eyes.

ARTICLE XII

IT'S ALWAYS THE PLAYOFFS:
Sports as Barrier to Intimacy & The Offensiveness of the Sports Metaphor

Men love sports. Women usually don't, but they try to love men, and sometimes that means putting up with sports.

Initially, a woman may feign a genuine interest in your beloved game, just to get close to you. She'll ask a lot of questions, and when you answer them, she'll be really happy: You're relating! Before long, she'll accompany you and your friends to the Garden, beating her breasts very convincingly as the Rangers bring home yet another one.

But even as she watches you glory in bodies crunching on rock-hard ice and bits of gore spattering onto the boards, she mistakenly believes she is leading you forward in a tender dance of intimacy. Later that night, when she wants to snuggle and talk about feelings, you are patrolling the bedroom, rambunctiously reenacting Messier's breakaway goal.

Your girlfriend will come to loathe your fandom—that carrot dangled before her hurrying Ferragamos, that place where you put all the fervor and loyalty and seriousness you should be reserving for her (we're assuming you're not faking your reverence for Saturday afternoon ESPN2 motocross).

But she will grimly tolerate your sports obsession. Tersely and urgently hissed, the magic incantation, "It's the playoffs!" has successfully warded off many an attempt to bewitch us into stirring the risotto, snuggling, or just talking. There's only one way to get a guy to stop watching the World Series.

Women who will watch sports with you may be grouped in three varieties. Don't trust a single one of them.

1. THE DILETTANTE

She never liked sports before, but she's suddenly caught up in the local enthusiasm for a playoff-bound team, and she likes feeling part of something communal, larger than herself. In this suddenly small metropolis, she shares a bond with her 2 million rooting neighbors, and with you and your male friends. It's a heady enchantment for her, a summer-into-fall miasma of ardent ignorance. It's kind of like her relationship with you, come to think of it.

You hardly wish to disturb her delicate dream. But you know that come January she won't give a rat's ass for the infield fly rule. As your indignation mounts, you resolve to put her off the scent. She's eager to learn (and, you well know, soon to forget). So you instruct her erroneously in the finer points of your beloved game: Baseball players chew tobacco because it makes them stronger. That last-second hook shot that never touched rim is a "squish." Every player who catches the football gets a prize at the end of the game.

At last the great day dawns: Game 7, hosted by a friend of yours she's never met. She's eager to trot out her newly acquired wisdom and gain entrance to your fraternity of fandom; during the playoffs, every stranger is a friend just waiting to meet you! Well, you've got some news for her: these strangers are *staying* strangers.

2. THE TUCHIS-WATCHER

You're watching the Series again. No sooner has the anthem been sung than she launches into a rhapsodic recitation of the physical virtues of one Andy Pettitte. You find yourself agreeing; somehow you're even flattered. It seems poetically apt to you that the gods of sports should be thoroughly godlike.

But in the bottom of the first inning, she applies herself just as industriously to the admiration of John Smoltz. It's a stunning betrayal. First of all, you don't find him particularly attractive. Second, he plays for the enemy. She's breached your trust—the Yankees' trust. She's no fan, she's a woman!

Well, God knows you can like John Smoltz just

as much as she can—more! You set about doing so. You make your amorous intentions known to him in a letter. You ask her to type it.

3. THE COSELL

She served as watergirl to the high school hoops teams of her four older brothers—all of whom subsequently played at Division I schools with planet-sized stadiums. At parties, she neatly steps in for you to gloss the distinction between team fouls and personal fouls. You know a lot about sports, but she knows *everything*. It's damned embarrassing; people are starting to talk.

If you're dating such a person, you have only one weapon in your arsenal: the sports metaphor. No figure of speech is less fresh, less evocative, less daringly romantic. Employ it during moments of high drama if you really want to impress a woman with your shallowness.

The next time you take her out to look at the stars, observe ruefully that the net between you can't be crossed—not during the match, anyway. She may be a control pitcher who works the corners, but you're from a family of placekickers. She's a mashie, you're a pitching wedge; it's all so impossible.

ARTICLE XIII

WHAT WOMEN'S LIB
REALLY MEANS

Men's lib.

ARTICLE XIV

"YOU'LL NEVER LOVE ME
AS MUCH AS YOU LOVE
THAT DOG":
Canine Meditations

A man walking his dog is a pretty picture indeed, conjuring in a woman's mind Kodachrome visions of a perambulating, stroller-pushing househusband with ribbons in his hair. Short of a clean apartment and a good job, nothing makes a man appear more marriageable than dog ownership.

Your daily stroll with that ready Ziploc in your pocket attests to your sense of responsibility and regularity of routine. Your stoop to scoop tubes bespeaks humility and a readiness to change the nastiest of diapers. When you briefly caress the bump at the crown of Otto's noble head, you call to mind the masculine tenderness of the bare-chested, baby-cradling, *married* Bruce Willis in *Vanity Fair.* It sure seems like you love that dog. And you do—more than you'll ever love her.

Like your dog, you have the instinct of a roamer, an explorer's unslakably curious heart. Like him, you need to meet new people regularly and have sex with them indiscriminately. Indeed, Otto helps you to understand the whole enterprise of noncommittal sex as both bold and wholesome, as if a long-lost series of paintings of strippers by Norman Rockwell had suddenly come to light.

Let's face it, nothing breaks the ice better than a humping pup. His adorably frenzied friendliness during your first meeting in the park puts the subject of sex where it belongs: at the top of the agenda. Next to his spastic desperation even you are a model of sexual decorum.

Women will tell you that they believe in fate, that nothing ever happens by accident, but if they knew the ruses we devise to meet them, dog-aided, they'd sing a different tune. A dog is an accessory to the crime of passion. You must obedience-train your accomplice until he is so well disciplined that he can take apart a rifle and put it back together again. A woman's good-natured laugh at an inquisitive snout's nether foray belies the hand command that instigated it from fifty feet away. She looks up to see two pairs of inquisitive nostrils, and it's hard to say which is cuter.

Don't panic when she starts thinking she's your girlfriend. Man's best friend will be her undoing; he is her chief competition in a battle for top billing in your affections. She considers herself a front-page story, yet she finds herself relegated to the inside of the A section, then to the Metro Section, and finally bumped to Business (see Chapter III: "But First the Consumer—You!"). This newspaper is missing a Home section! She's finding out the hard way that some animals are more equal than others.

Thus, your dog encroaches on her territory, wedging himself between her and you at moments of highest intimacy. It's a different thing entirely, she finds, to be crotch-sniffed in the nude. That high stroke-per-minute rate when you fondle his withers reminds her anxiously of something.

Once she starts to get the hint, up the ante. Don't ask her what she did at work that day; brood instead over the cruel neglect of Mother Nature, who deprived your dog of opposable thumbs. Beg off seeing her one night with the excuse that Otto playfully piranhaed your privates retrieving a tennis ball in your lap. She will have to ask herself, Does my boyfriend just need me for the sex? The answer, of course, is *of course*.

If necessary, go that extra step. When she calls and asks you to come over ("You'll never guess what I'm wearing"), tell her you have to walk Otto first. By the time you show up, hours later, she'll be crusty-eyed and shrouded in Lanz of Salzburg. Let her plan that romantic weekend for two, but bail on Friday when you "can't get a dog-sitter." Spend the weekend back at the park instead. . . .

Months later, she chances to pass by the window of your apartment and peers inside. You and the dog are sharing a steak burrito in front of a Classic Sports Network rerun of the Connors-Krickstein U.S. Open quarterfinal. She studies your faces in the flickering blue light of the television, looking from dog to man, and from man to dog, and from dog to man again; but already it is impossible for her to say which is which.

'Tis better to have loved and lost out to Otto the weimaraner than never to have loved at all. Isn't it?

Table III
Famous Code Girls

Jane Austen's Emma
Amelia Earhart
Elizabeth Taylor
Julia Roberts
The Wife of Bath
Courtney Love
Jackie Onassis
Moll Flanders
Camille Paglia
Madame de Pompadour
Lauren Hutton
Lady Macbeth
Theda Bara
Emma Thompson
Batgirl
Linda Fiorentino
Madonna
Alyssa Milano

LOCATION, LOCATION, LOCATION:
The No-Sex-in-Bed Rule

Okay, she's got Dixon Ticonderogas grinding into her backside and you into her front. Paper is flying everywhere, and her nipples feel kind of crinkly from the Liquid Paper you applied, clenching the brush between your teeth. Your knee keeps double-clicking on the mouse, the side of her face is squished against the monitor, and distant exotic web sites appear full-blown and astral, taking her places she's never dreamed of.

Cybersex is a new frontier, a heated desktop publishing venture that supersedes more posture-pedic locales. Knowing *The Code* is all about looking for somewhere off the old map. Radical travel can be suppressed, demonized, called funny names, but the seeker's heroic exhortation finds its own voice, even if it's the mad howling of Ezra Pound—overlooked sex therapist—resounding over our century: "Make it new." The *Code* guy knows that nothing ruins romance like old stanzas of seduction and familiar flight plans. Fly you to the moon!

The old milieu, the bedroom, is a tomb: cozy, serene, and unalterably familiar once you've spent enough time there. The bed is a chilly marble slab in the morgue for victims of any and all matrimonial malfeasance.

An American Literature of Admonishment cautions against tract homes, hedge trimmers, and dust ruffles. The bereft souls in the fiction of John Cheever, the whining unbearable sameness of suburban sex in John Updike, the desperately numb couples in William Kennedy's bleak upstate New York all speak to the revolutionary American claim that a bird in the hand can't even compete with two in the bush. This tradition of letters is dedicated, not to the ferocious intensity of love gone strange or the charged thrill of Lawrentian naked wrestling, but to the tedium of Andrew Lloyd Webber: Too much of the same thing for too long on the same stage.

In these theatrical terms, practicing *The Code* is a shift from the staid proscenium arch of your boudoir, replete with all its blandly conventional choreography, to a revolutionary thinking—the realm of avant-garde theater, thrust stages, audience participation. Launch your own Theater of the Absurd! Make it a happening! Ahead of his time, as always, Shakespeare spoke lurid volumes when he said, "All the world's a stage." Use it!

Whether you're a woodsy ranger type out to shock a few elk or some skateboard jockey pushing up against your dream dip behind the Dairy Queen, you know that life is always elsewhere. Your ardor is too large for confined spaces; you're eager to take it outside and ravish the great wide open. You are not alone in your occult learning. Epochal scientific studies like the *Kinsey Report* testify that life is more exciting in unfamiliar surroundings, though perhaps not behind the double-paned glass of some sex institute, being stared at by a peep-show habitué in a lab coat.

Yet with the oral dissemination of *The Code* gospel it has become increasingly difficult for a gassed-up sexmonaut to do something extreme and otherworldly. To aid you in your endless prowling for the new, let us steer you toward the offbeat, the exotic, the paranormal.

EXTREME NOOKIE

1. *Shabu Shabu for six.* The kitchen-sex scene in *Bull Durham* is the Happy Meal of carnality, the mock-cheerful profferings of bland burger tossers. Visiting the golden arches is an event if you're ten, but not if you've already hit all the priapic rides in McPlayland. Instead of that desultory domesticity, ride the pacific rim of pan-Asian sensuality with food imports. Make her your sashimi babe, the human bento box for your miso missile. Futo-maki!

2. *Apocalypse Now.* You *are* an assassin, sent by grocery clerks to collect a bill. Bushwhack across the jungle of your apartment toward

the dark heart of brutish desire. Wade through fetid swampland (tub), suspend her on thick vines (stairwell), and roll through tangled masses of vegetation (that dead ficus tree in the corner). Late in the film, when Kurtz asks Marlow what he thinks of his methods, Marlow replies, "I don't see any method at all." Exactly.

3. *The knee trembler.* Even more charged and frantic than coitus with a time clock (read "elevator sex"), is humping love's caboose on unsure footing: Put your buck and a half to good use, like an upright performance between cars of the D train at midnight barreling through the Bronx.

4. *Urban rappel.* Colossal bondage at heaven-kissing heights with ropes, cleats, and clamps. Scale the World Trade Center with the vigor of Sir Edmund Hillary first mounting Everest. Hey, what's that third tower?

5. *Bungee sex.*
YeeooooOOOOOooooooooooow!

The underlying point, of course, is that bedrooms are for beds, and beds are for sleeping. If the downy raft is your only dais of discovery, you are in for a love life exactly as variegated and exciting as that rectangle and its mutely patterned percales.

When the only piercing arias of pleasure are from sheets by Missoni, well, you get the point. . . .

"No sex in bed" is not a hard and fast rule—actually, that's exactly what it is. It is the rule of *Code* concupiscence, stamped by stealth, quickness, and flexibility. The oscillating yodels of an outward bounder drown out the sad lamenting strains of a Sealy under stress. More important, sex on the run doesn't even have to broach the most ponderous and nagging question since Hamlet's soliloquy: *Your place or mine?* Instead, climbing the cliffs and fjords of passion's chance potentially unites sex and death, but never resides in the prefab home of sex as death. Success, then, is not measured by her whispering "that was nice" and softly padding off to the loo, but by her panting, disoriented, and disheveled, "Do you see my other shoe?"

ARTICLE XVI

CONDOMS À LA CODE

Nothing funny has ever been said about condoms, and this Article is no exception: You need them, and they hurt.

ARTICLE XVII

NO TAMPONS IN THE MEDICINE CABINET:
Protecting Our Borders

In these anxious times, closet space is at a premium. The staggering growth of the fashion industry in the past ten years has thrown women into the most brutish of Hobbesian competitions, millions of them rushing dizzily around the globe, blown to and fro by the shifting winds of style, arms laden with ripped jeans, slip dresses, and anything else that was worn on the first season of *90210*. Where are they going to put all those new clothes?

With the signing of NAFTA, there's even more stuff coming into the country every day. Had Ross Perot advocated a massive national public works campaign to foster the building of closets in 1992, he would have *ruled* the female vote. Thanks to mid-priced franchise stores like Urban Outfitters and Banana Republic—their rapid expansion fueled by cheap labor from places like Fiji—it's never been so easy for chicks to buy lots of stuff and so hard for them to find a place to put it.

So when she leaves behind her Benetton sweater on your couch, it's easy to think she's just using you for your storage. Don't. Something far more insidious is going on.

Every bra, every wool scarf, every gym bag she can't carry to work the next day, every pair of sexy panties—each is a seed from which the swiftly growing, astoundingly tangled kudzu of her marital aspirations can take root and flourish. Relationships to a woman are all about growth—her own, but especially yours—and her belongings are the secret, stealthy encroachers of her domestic designs. It's not just the Belizean guy who made her cotton pullover who's being exploited. It's you!

Think in terms of magic realism. Left unattended on your floor, her solitary sock will creepingly lay claim to a full dresser drawer. The bristles of her spare toothbrush will sprout under cover of night and wind themselves around a shelf in your medicine cabinet. While you're away at work, the handle of an umbrella will rudely push aside the contents of an entire closet. Nothing can compare with the shock of your girlfriend's voice on the phone asking if the bra she can't find at home might be in "her" compartment of your freestanding wardrobe. Better check your border policy, because a lot of her immigrants are trying to get into the country of you!

Know this axiom and know it well: Anything she leaves behind is something she's coming back for. You can be sure that her one sock under the bed is going to send home for the rest of its family. Search the most obscure corners of your apartment every time she goes home, or you can kiss your privacy goodbye. She's phoning you right now: She needs her black tights for tonight (they're inside a hollowed-out copy of the phone book). The weather is so changeable this time of year! Lucky she happens to be meeting her friends in your neighborhood. And that her flannel pajamas are in your pasta pot.

Don't panic. You can work this out. With every article she deposits in your apartment, your girlfriend is conducting a test of your trustworthiness—a test you're going to flunk in a big way. Is your apartment a country she can live in? It's time to institute some public policy.

1. UNDOCUMENTED IMMIGRATION

She insists she left her muffler at your place (wrapped around a basketball in your sports chest). You say you never saw it. She can't provide proof of entry. Well, no matter; she bought it off the street, anyway. (Until it exploded in a shower of fake fur and plastic, the muffler imparted some pretty interesting aerodynamics to your half-court hook shot.)

2. ILLEGAL LABOR

Where's her toothbrush? She left it right next to yours. There's no paper trail, but your bathroom grouting is suspiciously lily-white.

3. OUR RACIST BORDER GUARDS CAN'T TELL THEM APART

Isn't that *her* bra? Oops. Well, she's welcome to it.

She asks you why her stuff keeps getting lost. Even if it isn't that big, you tell her, your apartment has a lot of provinces—bookshelves, racks, cabinets, desk drawers, the top of the TV. Not to mention the floor. In all that glorious (but cluttered) space, it can be easy for foreigners to lose their way. Remind her of the time you couldn't find your own blue suit (and it lives there!). You're sorry, but her things are outside the system. You just can't keep track.

TABLE IV
"HOW WAS I?":
THE POSTCOITAL REVIEW

Inevitably, your native taciturnity will drive her to solicit early reviews of her debut performance. To date, you have uttered fewer than a hundred words. Now is no time to let her stop projecting.

Your aim here is to deflect her question in such a way that she is driven on to even greater heights of erotic daring. Women love a challenge, or else they wouldn't date a guy like you in the first place. Among your options: confusing her; subtly offending; throwing a teensy bone.

So when she asks how it was for you, answer in this spirit:

1. "You make me feel like David Copperfield (not the magician)."

2. "There are a million stories in the naked city. Too bad we're not one of them."

3. "Oh, this'll blow over."

4. "I've never dated an accountant before."

5. "I'll have my people get in touch with your people."

6. "The house is on fire!"

7. "You're a pop top in a world of pull tabs."

8. "I know—next time, *you* move."

9. "John 3:16."

10. "Well, it's morning, and I still respect you."

HOW DO I *LIKE* THEE?

In any given relationship (for lack of a better word), there are certain moments that matter more than others. Among these are the first kiss, the first time you make love, the first time you meet her friends, the first present she gives you, or the first birthday of hers you forget. Each of these adds a certain emotional ballast to the relationship (sorry!), but can just as well fly by like mile markers on the way to Ikea if you're not paying attention to the mania you are involved in. Remember, concentrate: Anything *can* be taken lightly.

But one hurdle in this emotional steeplechase that you shouldn't blithely ignore is when you are asked to stand and deliver those three dangerous words: "I love you." The days sometimes have a way of zipping by with unremarkable regularity, but this day will have you feeling decidedly cap-in-hand if you are caught unawares. Understand the implications: this is not some imaginary crossing of barriers, but a shift from emotional South to North Vietnam. Say, "I love you," and the two of you will be picking out kitchen carpets and window treatments faster than you can say, "Men are from Mars, women are from Venus."

Clearly, her initial sword-thrust, her saying, "I love you," isn't a sentiment, but a *challenge,* one that asks if you're tough enough, man enough, to cross her line in the sand. Men who don't know *The Code* fall back on set patterns when their manhood is called into question and invariably create more problems than they solve.

Our friend Dick, for example, could never back down from a challenge. He played pro ball for the Steelers' defensive line and approached all of life with a tackle's narrowness of focus. He regularly turned small scuffles into big confrontations, and when his girlfriend slapped him with, "You don't love me!" he slapped back—with 2.5 carats. Poor sap is now off the gridiron and knee-deep in Huggies. Hit and hit back is not knowing *The Code;* it's thermodynamics.

Perhaps you're not a Dick. Since every situation is different, it can be difficult to know how to respond appropriately. Here are some sample responses so that you won't be caught unprepared the day she thrusts the first, "I love you."

1. *Loud Contradiction.* **"No, you don't!"** This can knock her back on her heels like a gale-force wind. She'll be pissed at you for a while, but will cool off quickly. (Possible tears.)

2. *The Heathcliff.* (No script.) Quickly grab her in a passionate clench, a muscled kiss of Olympic duration. The thought of further conversation is made ridiculous. This is the

"Don't Talk—Let Her Project" (see Article V) response that lets her think whatever she wants to, without you having to incriminate yourself. A sexy way to take the Fifth Amendment.

3. *The Judo Defense.* **"But what is love, anyway?"** Popularized by O. J. Simpson's lawyers, the Judo Defense turns the strength of the opening statement back on itself. By going to foundations, you call into question her careless use of such terminology.

4. *Apoplexia.* **"Ya-*hoo!*"** **"Yee-haw!"** **"Hot *damn!*"** Or any combination thereof, delivered with great athleticism. Particularly effective in public places; if you give no appearance of stopping, this stratagem will have her trying to quiet you and change the topic as quickly as possible. Seem sincere, not hostile: You want apoplexia, not Tourette's.

5. *The "Sweet & Low."* **"That is *so* sweet!"** **"You are *so* wonderful,"** etc. With this saccharine approach, you can kill her with kindness. Just be sure not to cross that line.

6. The Cartesian Double-Bluff. **"*Do* you?"** Delivered with a philosopher's pondering, this reply can inject a Cartesian doubt into the whole equation. A subtle, difficult parry

useful near the end of a relationship that, if correctly delivered, will take the focus off you and have her asking herself, *"Do I?"*

7. *Gaslighting.* **"You know how I feel."** Fight craziness with insanity. She can't possibly know how you feel. But if you make her feel like she *should* know, that *she's* the one that isn't paying attention, well, then, you're halfway home, aren't you?

8. *The My-Mind-Is-Elsewhere Approach.* **"God damn, those Red Sox!"** **"Now *that's* a deep-conditioning treatment!"** The non sequitur can be your greatest ally when your back is to the wall. A desperate recourse: To be sure, use it forcefully—and sparingly.

> ### ADDENDUM
>
> #### The Use and Abuse of the L-Word

Not to put too Machiavellian a point on this, but you don't want to look so stupid as to not even know the L-Word. In fact, a profligate use of it can keep her frustrated (women love to be frustrated!) and fixated on you. Sprinkle your conversation indiscriminately: "Boy, do I *love* potato chips!"

"I simply *love* my new refrigerator, it's so upright!" "Minted tooth floss is what I *love,* don't you?" To raise the stakes, make the air strikes a little closer to home: "My friends just *love* you!" Or, "My parents are going to *love* you when you meet them" (yeah, right!).

The one thing you have (well, okay, the other thing you have) is the one thing she wants, that magic trinity passing across your lips: "I love you." The second you give in is the second she is out of your thrall and on to carpet samples. Keep her there; foster that dependence. Dangle the word in front of her like a carrot, and she will pursue you until she gets it. To respond to her "I love you" with "I love you" lends a certain symmetry, a clarification, a balancing—and that's just not healthy.

ARTICLE XIX

EMOTIONAL PANHANDLING:
Rattling the Tin Cup of Intimacy

Every male-female relationship in life fosters a fierce competition for the title of "The Neediest." Any Darwinian worth his salt will tell you that when two people get together, it's a psychic Greco-Roman tussle. The loser will be tossed out of the ring of neediness. The winner gets whining rights. Even the average drinks date is an early positioning for pride of place, capable of defining the ultimate power-grab for attention.

When people are actively engaged in the stressful activity of a relationship, they may tend to lose track of time and other mundane concerns, easily obscuring the big picture. Since we know that big pictures always involve the twin evils of frank discussion and long-term planning, it is important to keep the picture small and sharply focused on you.

Girls love it when guys seem somehow inexplicably wounded. You *are* needy. Learn this invaluable truth, and learn it well: *The person with the most problems controls the relationship.* Don't be stupidly stalwart and parade your machismo; play up your flaws and witness her joyous and purposeful attempts to fix you. You can choose to be the car or the mechanic; which sounds like the better deal to you? Lie back like a big old Chevrolet and let her play Mrs. Goodwrench to her heart's content.

Once you've got her fragile raft far from the shore of self sufficiency, sink the depth charge: You want to *change.* Plead that you don't know why you feel the way you do, misdirected, purposeless, and hollow. Your misery knows no bounds, you can say; you don't know how you got this way.

After you've established this "broken man" syndrome, mooch as much sympathy as you can. Shoplift from the megamall of her munificence. She'll keep you afloat because her new-found identity depends upon it. She has learned that her

satisfaction is satisfying *you*. Sure it's manipula-
tive, but don't think she wouldn't jump at the
chance if she had the drop on you.

She'll be happy to pick up your dry cleaning on
the way home from work if it means she might
get a glimpse of you. She'll be even happier to
walk your dog (see Article XIV: "'You'll Never
Love Me as Much as You Love That Dog': Canine
Meditations") during the week you're "visiting
your sick aunt," which is to say, hunting oryx with
your homies in the green hills of Africa.

Weigh in with excess at every opportunity.
Never concede an inch. She's cold; you're *freezing!*
She has a headache; you have a *migraine* (and your
left arm feels oddly numb). Her parents divorced
when she was in college? Your parents deserted
you at age five—and all you inherited was
Hodgkin's disease!

With practice, you can twist even her worst
news to seem not quite as bad as yours, so go
ahead and twist. Yeah, it's terrible she was sacked.
But at least she doesn't have to sell her soul to cor-
porate America again, like you do, *tomorrow!*

Our friend Ron once had Saturday afternoon
plans that conflicted with his girlfriend's wishes.
Rather than accede to her request to go shoe shopping, he lay in bed all morning, refusing nour-
ishment and ignoring her efforts at cheerful
company. He murmured quasi-suicidal thoughts
whenever his girlfriend asked what he wanted to
do. "We could go see the string quartet in the

park," she chirped. "I can't," he groaned, "you go." She tried everything to bring him out of his stupor, gamboling and frolicking around the sides of his putative death bed, buoyantly enumerating various lively activities in the face of his dolorous mood and continued laments. "Well," he conceded finally, "we could, maybe, go to Wrestlemania XXXVII: Clash in Pandemonium." "Great," she wilted, concealing it was the last thing on earth she'd ever want to do on a Saturday, or any day. By then she'd have done *anything* to get out of the apartment—comforting herself that she'd pulled Ron back from the brink. Every woman is a Florence Nightingale just waiting to meet you. Call the nurse!

Applied constructively, even cerebrally, the long-term funk can be even more useful. Look worldly wise and tortured. Affect fin de siècle dyspepsia; call yourself Ishmael; quote liberally from Coleridge's "Ode to Dejection" and Burton's *Anatomy of Melancholy;* relate vividly to Hugh Grant's doleful, pained expression in any of the masterworks in his canon. Being up to date with current world crises is also a good way to defuse any of her bids to control the relationship. So those Manolo Blahniks pinch her toes. They're sexy; it's not like she has to flee a band of marauding Burundian Hutus. Sheesh!

Appearing to take the weight of the world on your shoulders will have her thinking that you are capable of some feeling, for someone, *somewhere.*

Someday, she'll think to herself, if I work really really hard, that someone could be ME!

You have trapped her in a sticky web of co-dependence. She'll never unravel it; when the time comes, you'll have to. You've been unfair to her; now you see it. She'd be happier with someone else; you can't force your suffering on her any longer. You need time to discover why you are so unhappy. You are taking her advice to see a therapist, the one *her* therapist recommended! "You must change your life," wrote the poet Rilke in *Letters to a Young Poet*. You always said you wanted to; now you are. You know you have her full support. Hug?

ARTICLE XX

WOMEN ARE NATURAL-BORN SPIES: *How to Incriminate Yourself Free*

TOP SECRET AND CONFIDENTIAL

TO: Code Headquarters
From: Panicked Agent

Sensing a cabal. Famke has been working covertly for some time now, but things are really heating up. Think she's trying to ring me into something nefarious.

Continuing with counter espionage: Read

glamour mags in her apartment and listened to her message machine when she pretended to "step out for milk" (came back empty-handed!). But this is small potatoes in the face of what she seems to be hatching. Saw her whispering with coconspirators; some red-haired agitator kept asking about my "potential." One dropped a sheaf of documents; on examination, a list of baby names! Sought counsel with the local Mata Hari, but could turn up next to nothing on Famke's cohorts or ultimate aim. Her history is murkier than Lee Harvey Oswald's—who *is* she working for? Could be in over my head on this one. What to do? Awaiting instructions.

TOP SECRET AND CONFIDENTIAL
TO: **Panicked Agent**
From: **Code Headquarters**

Cool your heels. You did the right thing contacting us. Duplicity got you into this, it can get you out.

Little has been turned up on "Famke" or Redhead from cross-referencing data banks, but you will survive this. Advise you to let her spy—every woman thinks it's her God-given right.

TOP SECRET AND CONFIDENTIAL
TO: **Code H.Q.**
From: **Panicked Agent**

Most unhelpful! I'm hanging my ass out here, and you're talking theology!?

I need help—*now!* I've eluded her so far, but it's a real dance-of-death with slyboots, let me tell you. Fearing I could end up in a black-and-white body bag faster than you can say cummerbund and shirt studs. Redhead has turned into an agent provocateur without peer; recon says she's part of some Tong run by Vera Wang.

Urgently need directions to safe house.

TOP SECRET AND CONTRADICTORY

TO: Panicked Agent

From: Code Headquarters

Are you really working for us? For this we spent good training dollars on you? Where did you put your notes from class? (Are they at risk?) Stop pretending to have good intentions, and do as we taught you: Blow your own cover. This is the last time we're going to convey the secrets of self-incrimination to you. Fail this mission, and we'll deny any knowledge of your existence; and you can kiss your *Code* commission goodbye.

Now, start by giving her the keys to your apartment. This shining display of your trust—which is how she'll read it—is your own Trojan Horse policy. If she hasn't already examined the recesses of your domestic booby trap, she will now.

Traffic in contraband: There should be photo albums with glossy prints of other double agents you've colluded with. She's a spy, after all, and it's only a matter of time before she knows the nooks and crannies of your apartment better than Sirhan Sirhan knows his cell.

A journal with descriptions of other foreign affairs should be hidden but findable.

Leave the access code for your voice mail cunningly exposed; she'll listen to every last call from the other spies who love you. She'll get the message.

Conspire with her doubts about your loyalty; rush her to indict you in her Star Chamber by "hiding" a list of her charms and faults. Be sure the "pros" aren't too pro, they should be artfully misguiding (remember "mixed messages" special training⸮). Special ops has prepared the following dossier to help you:

What I think of [her name here]:

Pros	Cons
she's athletic	laps me on the track
knows her way around a kitchen	keeps stealing my ski gloves and threatening me with knives
she's younger than me	she acts like a nine-year-old
she drinks like a fish	she pukes like a lumberjack

Pros	Cons
dances like Ginger Rogers	looks like Fred Astaire
she's tall	her head is the size of a pea
she smells good	she has a mouth like a toilet
she's a B-cup	she's a B-cup
good with her hands	eats with them
heart-shaped face	pear-shaped body
looks nice in candlelight	like my mother
gives good head (but who doesn't?)	doesn't swallow
likes my risotto (but who doesn't?)	eats *all* of it

Breaking up is hard to do—plant this information somewhere and let her do it.

TOP SECRET AND CONFIDENTIAL
TO: Code Headquarters
From: Panicked Agent

Played gambit perfectly. Also utilized Famke's rumor-mongering colleagues. Made sure to be seen by the subversive network with a leggy decoy. Within their earshot, I proffered to grease decoy's palm; she teasingly threatened to blow my whistle. Famke released me from my contract, once word leaked back, because I was "supporting a clandestine collaborator": Mission accomplished. Can we talk about my raise?

Table V
Enemies of *The Code*

Richard Nixon
Betty Friedan
post-1980 Jane Fonda
Alan Alda
Naomi Wolf
Robert Bly
Susan Faludi
John F. Kennedy, Jr.
The Lady Chablis
Hillary Clinton
Party of Five
Wendy Wasserstein
Tabitha Soren
John Gray
Andrea Dworkin
Hamlet
Bob Packwood
Miss Piggy
Bill Clinton
anyone who speaks ill of Alyssa Milano

ACCENTUATE YOUR INABILITY TO COMMIT AND OTHER CODE CONCEPTS FOR PERSONAL ADS

To a *Code* guy, a personal ad is a symphony of noncommitment performed in absentia, far removed from potential female fisticuffs. It's a revokable chess move; an Etch-a-Sketch erased with a quick, grainy shake; a disappearing line in the sand of the gender-war beachhead. No one knows who's authored a personal ad, whose free-floating desperation it expresses. It's a foray you never made, as far as the rest of the world is concerned—an innuendo you never proffered.

A *Code* guy personal ad must stay, like a debating would-be president, on message: I cannot commit, I cannot commit. A nontraditional overture, to be sure, and for some, a highly unmusical one. But there are those whose pulses will quicken, Geiger-like, in the presence of *Code* noncommitment. This is your niche market—know it, know it well, and use it often—married women (see Article XXIII: "Date a Married Woman"), back-of-magazine-perusers in shrink waiting rooms, relationship rebounders.

But do not take your audience for granted. Even the randiest woman has greater self-respect than a man in rut, and she will fend off your parley if it's not delivered with wit and style. After all, seduction has never been about substance.

In composing your waggish prelude to a kiss, a built-in escape hatch is essential. Relationships can suddenly burst into flames, your Bartle-byesque demurrings so many Duraflames tossed onto a bonfire of insanities. Know where the exits are! The following model personal ads should give you a sense of what we mean:

1. Kill me with kinky kindness! Autoerotic as-phyxiant seeks partner/onlooker for one-time-only joyride into oblivion.

2. Handsome, bare-chested Greek god residing by the sea seeks leggy, swan-throated goddess to share fun in the sun. Chains excite me, as do the vultures who visit me daily to eat out my liver. Come on baby, light my fire—I lit yours!

3. I ratted out Gotti!

4. Priapic party-boy actor and longtime rider of paternal coattails offers vaguely defined domestic position to the right breast-augmented nineteen-year-old, or whatever. Until we've screwed and you've talked about it on *Howard Stern,* you just haven't been to L.A.

5. It's not like I killed the Pope. I could not would not kill the Pope.

A *Code* personal ad distills male/female relations to their passionate essence. It's free love at a dollar a word. But beware! You may know where you stand (namely, nowhere near her), but sex has a way of bringing people close together—of cracking the palisades we erect around the principalities of our emotions. If you sleep with a woman, she might start liking you, and THAT you need like a hole in the head.

There's one additional peril associated with *The Code* personal ad—a fourth estate of respondents.

The woman we're thinking of saw your ad in *L.A. Weekly;* she inhabits a world shaded in noir desperation. She wears flowered sundresses and garter belts without underwear; her skin is inexplicably bruised. Her tangled, dirty-blonde tresses fall in a slithery cascade to her shoulders. She props herself on your knee as she applies her lipstick in the rearview mirror of her convertible. She wants something, she wants it bad, and she doesn't have the foggiest notion what it is. Nor does she care. She's a *Code* girl, the first you've ever met, and you think you might be falling in love.

Don't. You promised yourself you wouldn't let it get personal.

ARTICLE XXII

NEVER TRADE ANYTHING FOR SEX, UNLESS IT'S ORAL SEX

Hummers come in two varieties: the harrowing and the ear-splittingly miraculous. Who among us hasn't lain with passion's barracuda, the icicle scrape of her vulpine molars drowning us in tsunamis of salty anguish? Never before have the tracks of our tears been so excruciatingly inscribed. Fortunately, there are other fish in the sea.

When we find a woman who gives resplendently of her oral self, we are the sovereigns of pleasure's liquid chambers. Inevitably, we recollect Freud's allusion to the "oceanic" sensation of the womb. Sad to say, most men are exiles from that fleshly palace of completeness and peace, doomed wretches who expend the whole of their bitter, conflicted lives striving to regain the abrogated uterine throne.

Some will seek to recapture this vanished sense of oneness by hugging a tree; *Code* guys sweetly solicit hummers. We have found that superior fellatio makes us whole again; it is sex's *ne plus ultra,* a joyous return to the mythical days when the phallus was a scepter of ultimate power, an enchanted wand, a staff of life. We are once again knights, gladiators, Sun Kings; we are reinstalled in the seat of power. Indeed, if we're lucky, her dainty fingers are probing that seat.

But watch out: If fabulous oral sex is a nostalgic piece of our long-lost magisterial home planet, it is also *Code* Kryptonite, a toxic phenomenon capable of disabling our resolve, of erecting a two-bedroom A-frame on the highway of desire faster than a team of Mennonites. Every *Code* guy has his price, and it's the same price. There's nothing we won't do for a radioactive moustache ride. And that includes reciprocating.

Compliment her shamelessly after her inaugural solo flight. The idea here is to encourage repeat visits, and you've got to create some incentive. A response such as, "I'm speechless," is always appropriate, since it both adheres to and violates *Code* Article V ("Don't Talk—Let Her Project"). In its daring breach of your vow of silence, such a remark can only push her to greater heights of erotic oral derring-do. Meanwhile, its ambiguity summons flattery's evil twin, confusion, to lend you a hand (see Article IX: "The Only Message Is a Mixed Message"). Is "speechless" a good or a bad thing? Even if she asks, you can't answer: You're speechless! In these heady early days, you can still perplex her into thinking oral sex is something SHE wants to do. (You're kidding yourself if you think she really likes it.)

Know that the balloon ride of the oral honeymoon ends with a rude bump. She's worked to map your erogenous zones studiously and comprehensively; now she's got you by the *cojones*. It's time to say goodbye to the free samples. Sure, you could bail at this point, but the best blow job you've ever gotten is the one you're getting RIGHT NOW.

On nights when she's not willing, you drag yourself to her bedside, starving, hysterical, naked, horny as a guppy. You need a fix, and you're waiting for the Ma'am. You're marooned on a *Gilligan's Island* of your own desperate desire. She's smoking your crack pipe, but it's you who's gotten addicted. Get ready to see a lot of Joan Osborne concerts. We'd tell you to think hopeful thoughts, but a woman doesn't readily admit a certain extremity between her gums for too long without contemplating another one—and the ring that ought to be on it.

Your mission, should you choose to accept it, is to maintain yourself in her oral affections while simultaneously Saddaming the hell out of there. It's a task that unites the coercive charms of a Speaker of the House with the squinting shrewdness of a Moroccan carpet trader. Demands for blow jobs are a saliva-streaked slippery slope down to a relationship's demise. Yet of all inflatable slides leading from emergency exits, surely this is the sweetest. Know when NOT to say when.

Persist in your gross demands no matter how tired she says she is. What's the harm? Don't break up with a woman, exhaust her. You'll either end up on her tongue or out the door. Even if she performs her ministrations grudgingly, it's not like you can tell the difference between fresh and canned. So what if that marriage-minded bully Big Business is trying to crush your independent spirit; you're part of the *Code* union, remember? What do you want? Oral sex! When do you want it? NOW!

Deep down, she's touched that you still want her. Or at least you still want *that*. You renew your list of demands (demand?) even as the glow of your fervent advances is finally overtaken by the sharp light of day. Suddenly, she sees you not as you once seemed but as you are: a guy who's constantly bothering her for blow jobs. Now she regards you with utter contempt, which is as it should be.

As you pull out of her driveway, you make a note of her name: You think you'll meet again some day, when she's married, in an out-of-the-way bar where she won't run into anyone she knows. You're wrong.

ARTICLE XXIII

DATE A MARRIED WOMAN

Before a man can set about this wife-stealing business with any prospect of success, five things are essential. He must be as handsome as P'an An. His member must be at least as large as a

> *donkey's. He must be as rich as Teng T'ung, and reasonably young. Finally, he must have plenty of time on his hands, and almost endless patience. If you are possessed of all these qualifications, you may think of going in for this sort of entertainment.*
>
> —**Wang Shih-Chen**, *Chin P'ing Mei*

Chinese author of a sixteen-hundred-page pornographic magnum opus, Wang Shih-Chen was obviously a man with a *lot* on his mind. A distant forefather of erotic e-mail, Shih-Chen's martial artistry produced belles lettres that flew like Ninja stars of naughty noncompliance—silent, pointed, no return-receipt required. To this day, his illicit and lubricious musings continue to warm the wontons of desire.

Like an amorous *The Art of War,* his work exhibits a certain timelessness that is spot-on in its treachery and duplicitousness. Sure, you could fault him for not foreseeing the rise of the well-heeled cuckold, that underwriter of feminine indulgence, but we never professed to being too eager to spend lots of money anyway. We've already—and unabashedly, we might add—established that the *Code* guy is out for his muscular frenzy on the cheap (refer to Article IV: "Let's Meet for Drinks: The Non-date Date," or to your notes). Clearly Shih-Chen is speaking here of messing unapologetically with established norms, of transcending the bourgeois dictates of committed coitus, of running through the red lights of others' marital incarcerations at high speeds.

In so many ways, dating a married woman is the savvy investor's hedge, warranting limited amounts of time and money for optimum payoff. It is the quick-and-easy recipe for gourmet tastes, a lavish spread ripe with adventure, smothered with lusty letting go and served with only the most negligible and inconsequential of bills.

More to the point, married women are willing, they're hurried, they're flexible, and they expect nothing of you on any of the major holidays—any Epicurean's recipe for bodice tasting.

There is no lingering fear that she might think, "Oh God, this could turn into something!" Quite the contrary. Her husband is the guy with the bucks, you're simply the buck. The freedom afforded by a married woman's private furlough program guarantees an affair qualitatively identical, throughout its duration, to the first rhapsodic days of any other relationship: There is only beginning and an eventual end; no messy, complicated middle. As in the heady days of new-found love, you'll never hear any bad news, you won't have to patiently suffer through impossibly tedious stories about her family, and you don't have to regale her with impressive yarns involving famous people you've met (well, seen).

Sure, you may hear an occasional complaint about the insufferable tool she's married to, but what better time to put a finger to her lips and throw her down on a rented bed? So what if you're being used; have you really got a problem with that? We didn't think so.

Still not convinced? Then consider that dating a married woman also reinforces the intoxicating hypothesis—almost too heady to contemplate—that *nothing* is impossible. Einstein once said pointedly that just because something hasn't happened doesn't mean it can't. Perhaps he wasn't musing solely on the average woman's inclination to stray, but he was very absentminded, we understand. So make it happen; plunder the primrose path of possibility, for there is always plenty of possibility.

As if sheer chance weren't enough, take the explosive statistics of *The Hite Report,* suggesting, among other calamities, that something like 37.83 percent of married women have never achieved orgasm (refer back to Einstein!). Can marriage really do that for her? The mental saw horses go up immediately in the *Code* guy psyche, declaring quietly, though insistently: This is a work zone. Put on your tool belt and latex hard hat; there's emergency work to be done. Fire in the hole!

It may seem like a violation of *Code* etiquette but, unlike your average slide into a relationship with a bachelorette, hooking up with a married woman demands that you take *some* action, however limited. Locked in lives of central air and the minivan dream, they don't lurk in toney bars or stroll languorously past your table at Fatburger.

You have to find them. You have to flush them out of the privet hedges of respectability.

In the summer months, try hanging around pools during the work week (married women love lifeguards). When you spot a woman obviously thrashing and drowning in her fatal suburban filiation, strut over in your striped trunks and do some resuscitating.

In winter, whoosh and shush the chalet circuit. Melt into rich, leather sofas circling the fireplace and behold all the ski-shy ladies-in-waiting. A pair of crutches and a leg cast are a great conversation starter that will win you both interest and sympathy from the get-go (for further reading, see Article XIX: "Emotional Panhandling: Rattling the Tin Cup of Intimacy"). Play it right, and while Hubby Herbie is out on the slopes caressing the moguls, you'll be inside, next to a warm fire, doing the same damn thing. Pick your line of descent, ski bum, and descend.

Not all cuckolds, be forewarned, take their lumps lying down. All the better if you look to a fling with a married woman to nourish your inner James Bond, satisfying a penchant for disaster: the hotel tryst, secret pacts, and high-speed car chases. The stakes can be high. The *Code* mystique speaks of a life on the edge, courts disaster, recognizes that nothing perks up a relationship like a little gunfire. If you find yourself staring down a Saturday Night Special in the paw of Marvin the Wonder Accountant, recognize it's time for the ripcord, big-time. Your Mrs. Robinson didn't get into this because you're the only guy in the world; you just got in the wrong carpool. Read the road signs, or you won't know when to get out.

Our friend Stephano, unfortunately, rode on to an unhealthy conclusion. Ignoring Marvin's menacing threats, he was found floating in knee-deep water in the Gowanus canal, with a small minnow stuck in his gap-toothed grin. Tragic and avoidable, yes, but all the same, he clearly died with a smile on his face.

TABLE VI
"DO I LOOK FAT?":
TEN DISCOURAGING ANSWERS TO THE MOST FREQUENTLY ASKED QUESTION

WHAT YOU SAY	WHAT SHE HEARS
"Why, am I too thin?"	"You look fat."
"No, but your pantyhose might be too small."	"You look fat."
"Where are the other two tenors?"	"You look fat."
"I divide women into white mice and brown mice, and you're a brown mouse."	"You look fat."
"What part?"	"You look fat."

WHAT YOU SAY	WHAT SHE HEARS
"Godfather, I come to you in respect."	"You look fat."
"Why, is there any leftover risotto?"	"You look fat."
"I'm not sure. Spin for me."	"You look fat."
"It takes a big computer to save a long document."	"You look fat."
Shrug.	"He's never been with anyone fatter."

ARTICLE XXIV

NEVER ADMIT THERE IS A CODE

Break out the cigarettes and suntan lotion, because the interrogation lamp is shining on you. Your girlfriend has just asked you why you're acting like such a jerk. What are you going to say?

Surely you don't mean to suggest that there's an actual *system* underlying your behavior! What kind of guy would deliberately adhere to a policy of secrecy, withholding, connivance, manipulation, and deception just to get what he wants?

What guy wouldn't? But the aggravation you get for being honest—for once (what were you thinking?)—just isn't worth it. Don't ever admit to anyone that there's a *Code*. Not even your therapist. He or she might try to talk you out of it, and the strength of *The Code* is your completely unquestioning faith in it.

Don't just read *The Code*, burn incense and chant it. If anyone gives you any trouble, get together a thousand or so *Code* guys and some Kool-Aid. You know the drill.

ADDENDUM

AN INDEX OF NONCOMMITMENT: A LOT OF WAYS TO LEAVE YOUR LOVER

to shirk
to evade
to avoid
to run from
to dodge
to whiffle
to sidestep
to elude
to weasel out of
to shrink from
to blench at
to blink at
to sneak off
to sneak out the back
   way
to make oneself scarce
to take off
to take a walk
to play truant
to stay out
to shuffle off to Buffalo
to call in sick
to loaf
to malinger
to bail

to scrimshank
to cop out
to skip town
to see a better way
to sell short
to burrow out
to short-sheet
to beat cheeks
to flee
to head for the hills
to sunset
to retreat
to Saddam
to Hussein
to be with the wind
to moccasin
to duck and bob
to jib
to give the slip
to waffle
to fudge
to hedge
to backtrack
to tergiversate
to shilly-shally

to feint
to go AWOL
to slide
to jump ship

to skydive
to blow this pop stand
to ditch
to hit the bricks

ADDENDUM

TWELVE FOR THE OPEN ROAD: A DIRTY DOZEN

1. Never date a woman who can beat you up.

2. The Classic Sports Network is the ultimate *Code* channel—now it really is always the playoffs.

3. If you're going to leave her at the altar, leave with the cash.

4. You only have to give her one good massage. Promise more, and defer.

5. Pop quiz: If you don't know what affianced means, you need to find out.

6. If you ever find a woman who can put on a condom with her mouth, marry her.

7. Don't be alarmed by her biological clock.

8. *Code* underwear: nothing. You're combat-ready.

9. Every woman shtups to conquer.

10. If you don't have a dog, steal one.

11. No woman ever wants to look "nice."

12. Never pee in the street on a first date.

Now that you've read *The Code,* there are many reasons why you might need to have your name and address on your person. Note this information on this page and carry it in your wallet.

NAME:

ADDRESS:

PHONE NUMBER:

AGE:

BLOOD TYPE AND/OR ALLERGIES:

IF THERE'S STILL TIME, DO YOU NEED A PRIEST?:

The writers of *The Code* cannot be held responsible for any bodies found bent, spindled, mutilated, or floating.

ACKNOWLEDGMENTS

The authors would like to acknowledge the unfailing encouragement and wisdom of Amy Scheibe, *Code* girl deluxe. Without her, this book would not have been written.

For their generosity and support, we would also like to thank our literary agent, Janis Donnaud; our editor, Caroline Sutton; Bob Cooper; Benjamin Dreyer; Clare Ferraro; Sue Fleming-Holland; Peter Gethers; Mark Gompertz; Aviva Goode; Scott Greenberg; Nina Phillips; Jesse Sheidlower; Nan Shipley; Michael Siegel; and Trish Todd.

ABOUT THE AUTHORS

NATE PENN and LAWRENCE LAROSE live and work in New York City.